Programming in C

Evincepub Publishing

Parijat Extension, Bilaspur, Chhattisgarh 495001

First Published by Evincepub Publishing 2018

Copyright © Dr.Tanmay Kasbe 2018

All Rights Reserved.

ISBN: 978-93-88277-28-0

Price: Rs.300/-

This book has been published with all reasonable efforts taken to make the material error-free after the consent of the author. No part of this book shall be used, reproduced in any manner whatsoever without written permission from the author, except in the case of brief quotations embodied in critical articles and reviews. The Author of this book is solely responsible and liable for its content including but not limited to the views, representations, descriptions, statements, information, opinions and references ["Content"]. The Content of this book shall not constitute or be construed or deemed to reflect the opinion or expression of the Publisher or Editor. Neither the Publisher nor Editor endorse or approve the Content of this book or guarantee the reliability, accuracy or completeness of the Content published herein and do not make any representations or warranties of any kind, express or implied, including but not limited to the implied warranties of merchantability, fitness for a particular purpose. The Publisher and Editor shall not be liable whatsoever for any errors, omissions, whether such errors or omissions result from negligence, accident, or any other cause or claims for loss or damages of any kind, including without limitation, indirect or consequential loss or damage arising out of use, inability to use, or about the reliability, accuracy or sufficiency of the information contained in this book.

PROGRAMMING IN C

By

Dr. Tanmay Kasbe

ABOUT THE AUTHOR

Dr. Tanmay Kasbe is an MCA, PhD with over of 10 years of experience in academic and 6 years of experience in software industry. He has a long experience of teaching graduate, postgraduate and engineering students. A prolific writer, Mr. Tanmay has authored many research papers in international journals and presented research papers in many international conferences including IEEE & Springer in area of fuzzy expert system.

He has authored of "DBMS Concepts- A Practical approach" & "An Object Oriented Programming with C++"

About The Book

The C programming language is one of the most widely offered courses at many institutions and universities in the undergraduate programmers (all branches of BE, BSc Computer Science, and BCA) as well as various postgraduate programmers courses (MCA, MSc Computer Science), and the book is designed to cover all topics of DAVV university, Indore for B.Sc. Students. This book cover complete syllabus of B.Sc. first year students of DAVV. Beside, this book is also helpful for BCA students and this book also cover maximum syllabus of BCA students according to new yearly syllabus of DAVV.

Key features:
- Explain each and every topic unit wise according to first year BSc syllabus.
- Step by step guidelines for development of a program.
- 50+ programs with output.
- All the programs executed on Turbo C++ 4.0 compiler.
- 25 Objective questions with answer keys.
- 2 Model Question papers, according to new yearly pattern of BSc students.

Dedicated to my family

&

My Students

PREFACE

The book **'Programming in C'** has been written to meet the requirements of the students of B.Sc. first year of Devi Ahilya Vishwavidyalaya, Indore (MP). The topic covered in the book is strictly according to the new syllabus of the university.

Each Unit is organized in the way to clear the examination as well as students can gain a practical knowledge of the subjects. It is also a valuable reference for those enrolled in elementary courses in information technology and computer science.

I hope that the book will prove to be very useful for the student & teachers. Inspite of all the effort some error might be there.

Any Suggestion & Criticism for improvement is welcome & highly appreciated.

September, 2018

Tanmay Kasbe

tanmay.kasbe@gmail.com

Department of Higher Education, Government of Madhya Pradesh
Yearly Syllabus for Undergraduates
As recommended by Central Board of Studies of Computer Science and
Approved by H E the Governor of M.P.
Session 2017-2018

B.Sc. Ist YEAR COMPUTER SCIENCE
PAPER II: PROGRAMMING IN C

Max Marks: 42.5   Min Marks: 15

UNIT-I

Classification of programming language: procedural languages, problem oriented languages, non-procedural languages. Structured programming concepts: modular programming: top-down analysis, bottom-up analysis, and structured programming. Problem solving using computers: problem definition and analysis, problem design, coding, compilation, debugging and testing, documentation, implementation and maintenance.

UNIT-II

Introduction to C language: constants, variables, keywords, data types, operators, expressions, operator precedence and associatively. Structure of C program: variable declaration, declaration of variable as constant.

UNIT-III

Managing input/output Operators: Formatted and Unformatted. Control Statements: Branching. Jumping & Looping. Scope Rules, Storage Classes.

UNIT-IV

Arrays (one and two dimensional). Functions: user defined function, standard function, categories in functions, passing arguments to a function, recursion. Pointers: operators, declaration, pointer to arithmetic. array of pointers. Structures: declaring, accessing, initializing, array of structures.

UNIT-V

File handling in c: opening and closing a data file, inserting data to data file. **Graphics programming** -introduction, functions, stylish lines, drawing and filling images, palettes and colors, justifying text, bit of animation

Table of Contents

UNIT-I: Introduction to Programming Language

1.1 Introductions…………………………………………..1
1.2 Classification of Programming Language………….3

- ✓ Low Level Programming Language
  - Machine Language
  - Assembly Language
- ✓ High Level Programming Language

1.3 Procedural and Non-Procedural Programming….....7
1.4 Structure Programming……………………………..9
1.5 Top-Down & Bottom-Up Analysis……………….10
1.6 Problem Solving using Computer………………...14

- ✓ Problem Definition
- ✓ Problem Analysis
- ✓ Problem Designing
- ✓ Coding
- ✓ Compilation
- ✓ Debugging & Testing
- ✓ Implementation & Maintenance

UNIT-II: Introduction to C Language

2.1 Introductions……………………………………17
2.2 Translator Program………………………………..18

- ✓ Assembler
- ✓ Compiler
- ✓ Interpreter

2.3 Tokens in C...23
2.4 Data types in C.. 35
2.5 Expression & Statement...40
2.6 Structure of C Program..42

UNIT-III: C Basic Programming & Control Statement

3.1 Basic of C.. 44
3.2 Header file and Input / Output Functions............48
3.3 First Program in C......................................…...53
3.4 Control Statements.......................................…..61
- ✓ Decision Making / Branching
- ✓ Selection Statement (Switch)
- ✓ Iteration / Loop Statement
- ✓ Jump Statement

3.5 Scope Rules..…...86
3.6 Storage Class..…96

UNIT-IV: Array & Functions

4.1 Array Introductions...100
4.2 One Dimensional Array.................................. 101
4.3 Two Dimensional Array.................................. 109
4.4 Functions Introductions................................... 115
4.4 Recursion.. 135
4.6 Pointers... 145
4.7 Structure... 154

UNIT-V: File Handling & Graphics Programming

9.1 File Handling Introduction............................…163
- ✓ Opening & Closing File
- ✓ File Program Examples

9.2 Graphics Programming.................................... 170

- ✓ Graphics Program Example

APPENDIX-A: Objective Questions with Answer Key

UNIT - I

INTRODUCTION TO PROGRAMMING LANGUAGE

1.1 Introduction

A **software programming language** is a special language, which is used by programmers to create software programs or other sets of instructions for computers to execute. These commands can be interpreted into a code understood by a machine. Programs are created through programming languages to control the behavior and output of a machine.

As we all know computer cannot understand anything, for everything we must provide a set of instruction which is executed by programming language & then provide us an output. All the instruction which we have writes using any high level programming language is called **source code**. Most of the programming languages use translator programs to translate instructions into computer specific language.

A programming language is typically divided into three elements:

- ✓ Syntax
- ✓ Semantic
- ✓ Logic Developments

Syntax –

Like human languages, each programming language has its own grammar and syntax. In computer programming language it is very important to follow complete syntax otherwise it will not execute. A translator program responsibility is to check whether our program follow all the syntax of the language or not. If any mistake found by translator program then translator program will give errors and we must remove all the error then only our program will execute successfully.

Syntax deals solely with the form and structure of symbols in a language without any consideration given to their meaning. Each programming languages has its own syntax.

If we take some of the C programming language syntax likes –

; **(Semicolon)** used or represent end of line.

== **(Double Equals)** means when we have compared two values

X ++ means we have increase the value of **X** by **1**

Semantics –

Semantics describes the behavior that a computer follows when executing a program in the language. We might disclose this behavior by describing the relationship between the input and output of a program or by a step-by-step explanation of how a program will execute on a real or an abstract machine.**Semantics** follow directly from **syntax** .**Semantics** deal with the meaning assigned to the symbols, characters and words.Syntax is what the computer understands; semantics is what the human understands.

Examples:

- ➢ The sentence "Baby milk drinks" does not have a syntactic meaning, but through semantics most people would interpret it as meaning "Baby drinks milk "as our prior knowledge tells us that a baby drinks milk, and therefore we can find a meaning from the key words.
- ➢ In Database 'NULL' means when we don't know any value then it will set by default.

Logic Developments:

It is completely different from the syntax & semantic behavior of any programming language but it is the most important part of software development process. For every program or any software development,

Logics play an important role. We must bind our logic into syntax of particular language.

Logics are always same in all kind of programming language. Suppose we want to add two value, then we have always use + operator between two values. May be syntax of two different languages is different but logic is always same. If anyone wants to become a good software developer or programmer then their logics must be highly strong.

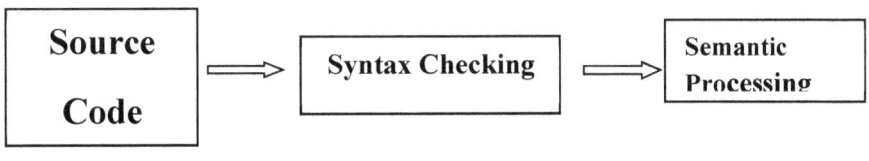

Fig. 1.1

1.2 Classification of Programming Language

There are three levels of computer programming languages –

- ✓ Low Level Programming Language
  - Machine Language
  - Assembly Language
- ✓ High Level Programming Language

Machine Language

Machine language is the lowest-level of programming language& it is also called 1G Programming Language. Machine language is a programming language that is interpreted and understood directly by the computer.

While easily and directly understood by computers, machine languages are almost impossible/difficult for programmer to use because they consist entirely of numbers. Machine language is consisting of 0's and 1's. They can understand only 0, 1, or combinations of 0 &

UNIT-I   Introduction To Programming Language

1. <u>Programmers</u>, therefore, use either a high-level programming language or an <u>assembly language</u>.

For example a program instruction may look like this -

1011000111101 , 1100101 , 10001010 , 10101010 , 1101

It is not an easy language for you to learn because of its difficult to understand. It is efficient for the computer but very inefficient for programmers. It is also difficult to debug the program written in this language.

Advantages

1. The only one advantage of ML is that program of machine language run very fast because they directly executed & interpreted by CPU.

Disadvantages

1. Machine code instructions still depend on the computer's architecture or computer's hardware so it is difficult to manage for programmer.

2. The programmer has to remember a lot of codes to write a program which results in program errors.

3. It is difficult to debug (Checking the code line by line) the program.

Assembly Language

Assembly Language is another low-level but very important language in which operation codes and operands (x,y..a,b) are given in the form of alphanumeric symbols instead of 0's and 1's. These alphanumeric symbols are known as **mnemoniccodes** and can combine in a maximum of five-letter combinations for example ADD for addition, SUB for subtraction, LD for loads, ST for store, START, LABEL etc. Because of this feature, assembly language is also known as 'Symbolic Programming Language.'

Assembly programming language is used for microprocessors and other programmable devices. It is not just a single language, but rather a group of languages. Assembly language implements a symbolic representation of the machine code needed to program a given CPU architecture. Each type of CPU has its own machine language and assembly language, so an assembly language programwritten for one type of CPU won't run on another. In the early days of programming, all programs were written in assembly language so it is also called 2G Language.

Example:

>LD R5, [Price]
>LD R6, [ShippingCharge]
>ADDI R0, R5 R6
>ST R0, [TotalCost]
>HLT

Advantages

1. Assembly language is easier to understand and use as compared to machine language.

2. It is easy to locate and correct errors, it is easily modified.

Disadvantages

1. In assembly language program is very long so it is hard for developer to remember.

2. It is machine dependent programming language.

3. Since it is machine dependent, the programmer also needs to understand the hardware.

High Level Programming Language

HLL (high-level language) is a computer programming language which is machine independent and isn't limited by the computer, designed for a specific job, and is easier to understand. It is more convenient programming language. It is more like human language and less like machine language. However, for a computer to understand and run a program created with a high-level language, we must use a translator program is called compiler.

High-level languages are basically symbolic languages that use English words and/or mathematical symbols rather than mnemonic codes. First HLL was developed in 1950. There are lots of HLL programming languages like C,C++,.NET, JAVA, PHP. Each & every programming language has its own syntax but logic is almost same in all programming language, you just follow syntax of particular language.

Advantages

1. High-level languages are user-friendly.

2. They are similar to English words and use English vocabulary and well-known symbols. HLL is also used mathematical symbol like + , - .

3. They are problem-oriented rather than machine oriented.

4. A program written in a high-level language can be translated into machine languages and can run on any computer.

5. Programs developed in a high-level language can be run on any computer text.

6. HLL take a less storage space in computer memory.

Disadvantages

1. A high-level language must translate into the machine language by a translator program, which takes up time so it slows as compared to ML & AL.

2. The object code generated by a translator program is might be inefficient compared to an assembly language program.

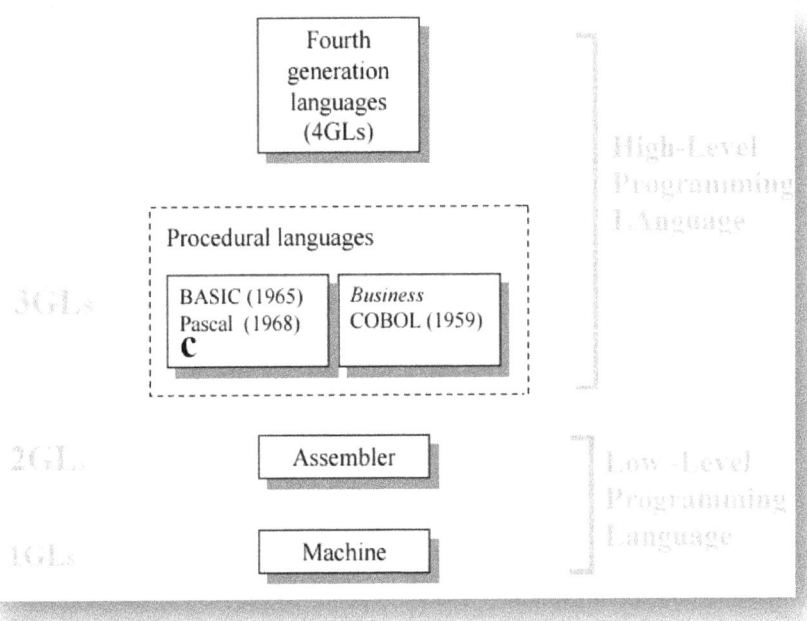

Fig. 1.2

1.3 Procedural & Non-Procedural Programming Language

In **procedural languages** a program is written as a sequence of instructions. We have to specify what to do and how to do. For example,

In C Programming before addition of two numbers, we must declare variable and then can use formula. In procedural languages a program will tell the whole step by step procedure to perform a particular task or job. So we provide a sequence of instructions and these instructions are executed in the given specified order. These instructions are written in order to solve a specific problem. Procedural languages are also called 3rd Generation languages or 3GL.

Example Are: C Language, COBOL, BASIC, PASCAL, FORTRAN

In **non-procedural languages** we have to specify only "what to do" and not "how to do". For example, SQL (structured query language) is a non procedural language. It is used in database systems.

Non Procedural languages are Fourth Generation Languages called 4GLs. In Non procedural languages we do not have to write whole set of instructions according to the logic of the program. But only one statement may be enough in a non procedural language to perform the whole job, for example select statement of SQL. Another example of non procedural languages is RPG.RPG stands for Report Program Generator. It is used for generating professional business reports.

Difference between Procedural Language & Non-Procedural Language

Procedural Language	Non Procedural Language
Procedural language directs the computer what to and how to do	Non-Procedural language directs the computer what to do not and how to do.
It is difficult to learn.	It is easy to learn.
It is difficult to debug.	It is easy to debug.
It requires large number of procedural instruction.	It requires a few non-procedural instructions.
It is normally used by professional programmers.	It can be used professional and non-technical users.
It is typically file-oriented.	It is typically database-oriented.

Procedural language provides many programming capabilities.	Non-procedural language provides less programming capabilities.
C, PASCAL, COBOL & BASIC are examples	SQL, RPG are examples.

1.4 Structure Programming / Modular Programming Concept

Structured programming (sometimes known as *modular programming*) is a subset of procedural programming, It is a programming method which aimed at improving quality, clarity and access time of computer program by the use of block structures, subroutines, for and while loops.

Structured programming is a software development method that uses modularization and structured design. This means that large programs or scripts are broken down into smaller modules and each individual module uses structured code, which means that the statements are organized in a specific manner that minimizes errors and misinterpretation. As its name suggests, structured programming is done in a structured programming language and PHP, C#, C++, Java, Visual Basic, and Python are such languages. The structured programming concept was formalized in 1966 by CorradoBohm and Giuseppe Jacopini. They demonstrated theoretical computer program design using sequences, decisions, and iterations.

This programming feature will be helpful when concept of exception handing is needed in the program. It uses various control structures, sub routines, blocks and theorem. The theorems involved in structure programming are Sequence, Selection, Iteration and Recursion. Most of the programming language uses structured programming language features such as ALGOL, Pascal, PL/I, Ada, C, etc.

Why C – Language is called as Structured Programming language?

C is called a structured programming language because it can solve a large problem; C programming language divides the problem into smaller modules called functions or procedures each of which handles a particular responsibility. The program which solves the entire problem is a collection of such functions.

Good example is calculating student's grade. Program is divided into these sub modules - input student marks, get student record, update student record, display student record, calculate grade. Here is a structural view of the program.

Advantages

- Structured programming is simple and easy to understand and implement.
- It is well suited for small size implementation. However this is not restricted. A good design can extend it to large size implementation.
- Programmers do not require knowing complex design concepts to start a new program.

Disadvantages

- Data and methods and not be bind together in a module.
- Polymorphism and inheritance are not available.
- Complex design and full object oriented design cannot be implemented.
- Programmers generally prefer object oriented programming language over structured programming language when implementing a complex gaming applications or front end business application

1.5 Top-Down & Bottom-Up Analysis

In Top-Down approach, a large task/ project divides into small parts, and these programs are known as modules and this approach is called top-down approach. It is also known as a specialization.

C programming language supports this approach for developing programs. It is always good idea that decomposing (Breaking) solution into smaller parts in a hierarchal manner.The basic task of a top-down approach is to divide the problem into tasks and then divide tasks into smaller sub-tasks and so on. In this approach, first we develop the main module and then the next level modules are developed. This procedure is continued until all the modules are developed.

Advantages

1. In this approach, first, we must create main or important module.
2. This approach is easy to see the progress of the task by developer or customer.
3. Using this approach, we can utilize computer resources in a proper manner according to the task.
4. Testing and debugging is easier and efficient and simpler.
5. In this approach, task implementation is shorter.

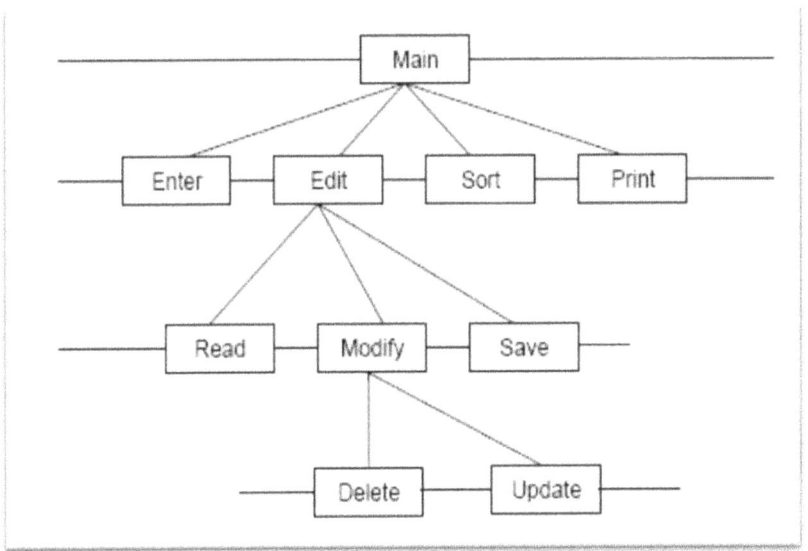

Fig.1.3

In Bottom-Up approach, bottom/lower level modules developed first (Lower level module developed, tested and debugged). It is an alternative approach to the top-down approach.

UNIT-I   Introduction To Programming Language

We can say that this module is also known as specialization. After creating the lower module then the next module developed, tested and debugged. This process is continued until all modules have been completed. This approach is exactly opposite to the top-down approach. This approach is good for reusability of code. C++ is the example for this approach.

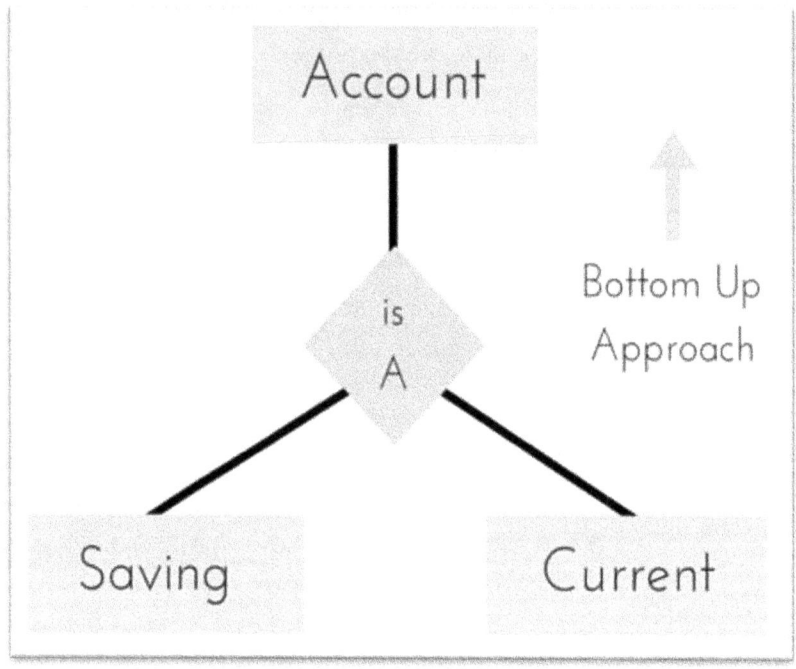

Fig.1.4

Top-down Approach	Bottom-up Approach
A top-down approach is breaking down of a program into its compositional small program (or module) in a reverse engineering fashion.	A bottom-up approach is the piecing together of module (or small program) to give rise to more complex program, thus making the original modules of the emergent program.
Structure / procedure oriented programming languages like C programming language follows top-down approach.	Object oriented programming languages like C++ and JAVA programming language follows bottom-up approach.
A top-down approach begins with high level design and ends with low level design or development.	A bottom-up approach begins with low level design or development and ends with high level design.
In top-down approach, main function is written first and all sub functions are called from main function thus, sub-functions are written based on the requirement	In bottom-up approach, code is developed from modules and then main function is developed.

1.6 Problem solving using computers

Problem Definition

Before a program is written for solving a problem, it is important to define the problem clearly. For most software projects, systems analysts approach system users to collect user requirements and define the problem that a system aims to solve. They typically look at the following issues:

- What is the problem?
- What is the input required for supporting the solution process?
- What is the expected output of the solution?
- How do people solve the problem currently?
- Can the problem or part of the problem be more effectively solved by a software solution?

Problem Analysis

If we are to use the computer as a problem-solving tool, then we must have a good analysis of the problem given. Here are some suggested steps on how to go about analyzing a certain problem for computer application:

1. Review the problem carefully and understand what you are asked to do.

2. Determine what information is given(input) and what result must be produced(output).

3. Assign names to each input and output items.

4. Determine the manner of processing that must be done on the input data to come up with the desired output(i.e., determine what formulas are needed to manipulate the given data).

Problem Design

As we have already discussed in this unit about Top-Down & Bottom-Up design.

Coding

In programming, code (noun) is a term used for both the statements written in a particular programming language - the source code, and a term for the source code after it has been processed by a compiler and made ready to run in the computer - the object code. Coding is the primary method for allowing intercommunication between humans and machines.

Early coding was done through physical punch cards and similar methods. As digital computers were created, early programming languages like BASIC, FORTRAN and COBOL were used, each with its own syntax and operators.

In C Programming Language, We have used Turbo C++ editor for programming and for making a program, we must write a proper code. Every code must follow the programming language syntax.

Compilation

We will discuss about compilation in next section (Translator Program.) of this unit.

Debugging and Testing

On successful culmination of software testing, debugging is performed. Debugging is defined as a process of analyzing and removing the error. It is considered necessary in most of the newly developed software or hardware and in commercial products/ personal application programs. For complex products, debugging is done at all the levels of the testing.Debugging is a developer activity and effective debugging is very important before testing begins to increase the quality of the system. Debugging will not give confidence that the system meets its requirements completely but testing gives confidence.

Debugging is considered to be a complex and time-consuming process since it attempts to remove errors at all the levels of testing. To perform debugging, debugger (debugging tool) is used to reproduce the conditions in which failure occurred, examine the program state, and locate the cause. With the help of debugger, programmers trace the program execution step by step (evaluating the value of variables) and halt the execution wherever required to reset the program variables. Note

UNIT-I Introduction To Programming Language

that some programming language packages include a debugger for checking the code for errors while it is being written.

Testing	Debugging
The purpose of testing is to find bugs and errors.	The purpose of debugging is to correct those bugs found during testing.
Testing is done by tester.	Debugging is done by programmer or developer.
It can be automated.	It can't be automated.
It can be done by outsider like client.	It must be done only by insider i.e. programmer.
Most of the testing can be done without design knowledge.	Debugging can't be done without proper design knowledge.

Implementation and Maintenance

Program implementation is actual implementation of your logic into code. It is a step after created logic for any problem. In this phase, we have used program syntax; variable declaration and all important code which is require executing code.

In software field, only implementation is not concern but it is also important how our code is executed. Because for one problem, maybe there are more than two solutions exist but thing is which is better and flexible solution. For example, In C programming, we have implemented prime number program in 3-4 ways. But we can use or implement that logic which works good and provide better output in every situation.

UNIT - II

INTRODUCTION TO C LANGUAGE

2.1 Introduction

C programming language is one of the most important language and we can say that it is a basic programming language and without knowledge of C programming, it is difficult for anyone to learn C++, Java or NET.

C is a General-Purpose / Procedural programming language, and is used for writing programs in many different applications, such as operating systems, graphical applications, etc. It is a small programming language, with just 32 keywords. It was initially developed by Dennis Ritchie at AT&T Bell Labs, between 1969 and 1973. It was mainly developed as a system programming (UNIX) language to write operating system. The main features of C language include low-level access to memory, simple set of keywords, and clean style, these features make C language suitable for system programming like operating system or compiler development.

Some Important Fact about C Programming Language:

- ✓ C Is called Middle Level or Structured Programming Language.
- ✓ C has been written in assembly language.
- ✓ LINUX/ UNIX, PHP and MySQL are written in C.
- ✓ The language was formalized in 1988 by the American National Standard Institute (ANSI).
- ✓ C is a successor of 'Basic Combined Programming Language' (BCPL) called B language.

For writing a C program you will need only two tools: a text editor, and a compiler. A C program is called "source code" and can be written using TURBO C++ or DOSBOX that you have handy; Simply type in your code and save it with a .c extension, then compile and link the code (linking is usually done automatically by the compiler and is a process of combining the source code with certain predefined functions, turning the .c program into an .obj file, and finally into an .exe file,) which makes the original .c program into a series of machine language instructions that can be used (executed) by the computer.

Uses / Application of C:

Some examples of the use of C might be:

- ✓ Database Systems
- ✓ Language Interpreters
- ✓ Compilers and Assemblers
- ✓ Operating Systems
- ✓ Network Drivers
- ✓ Embedded Systems

Features of C Programming Language:

- ✓ C is highly portable; programs once written in C can be run on other machines with minor or no modification.
- ✓ Programs written in C are efficient and fast.
- ✓ C is a collection of C library functions; we can also create our function and add it to the C library.
- ✓ C is easily extensible.
- ✓ C uses compiler to check code.

2.2 Translator Program

A translator program is program which translates our code into machine level code. As we have already discussed, Computer can understand only machine level language which is in form binary number system. So if we have create any program is HLL then we must required a translator program for converting our code into machine level.

Basically there are three types of translator program –

- ✓ Assembler
- ✓ Compiler
- ✓ Interpreter

Before explaining all three translator program we must know some important terms related with programming language which describe below:

Source Code:

Source code is a code where we have written all program logic with syntax. Every source code file save in particular file extension like C Program is save as .C , C++ Program is save as .C++ , C# program is save as .CS.

Object Code:

When a computer is executing set of instruction then it is called object code which is stored in computer memory components. The computer's control component takes the object code stored as a string of binary bits (i.e. 0's and 1's).

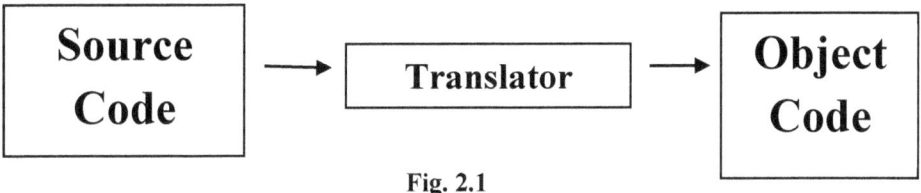

Fig. 2.1

Assembler

An assembler is translator program which translate assembly language into the machine language code.

If an assembler which runs on a computer and produces the machine codes for the same computer then it is called **self assembler** or resident assembler. If an assembler that runs on a computer and produces the machine codes for other computer then it is called **Cross Assembler**.

Fig. 2.2

Advantages

1. Assembler is faster in translating into machine code because it is 1:1 relationship.
2. Assembly code is very efficient because it is low level language.

Disadvantages

1. Most of assembly code is needed to do relatively simple tasks, and complex programs require lots of programming time.
2. Incompatible with other computer hardware because assembly language depends upon computer hardware.

Compiler

Compiler is a translator program which translates a high level programming language into a machine language code. A compiler is more intelligent than an assembler. It will checks all kinds of syntax errors, ranges etc. But its program run time is more and occupies a larger space of the memory. It has slow speed. Because a compiler goes through the entire program and then translates the entire program into machine codes. If a compiler runs on a computer and produces the machine codes for the same computer then it is known as a **self compiler or resident compiler**. On the other hand, if a compiler runs on a computer and produces the machine codes for other computer then it is known as a **cross Compiler**.

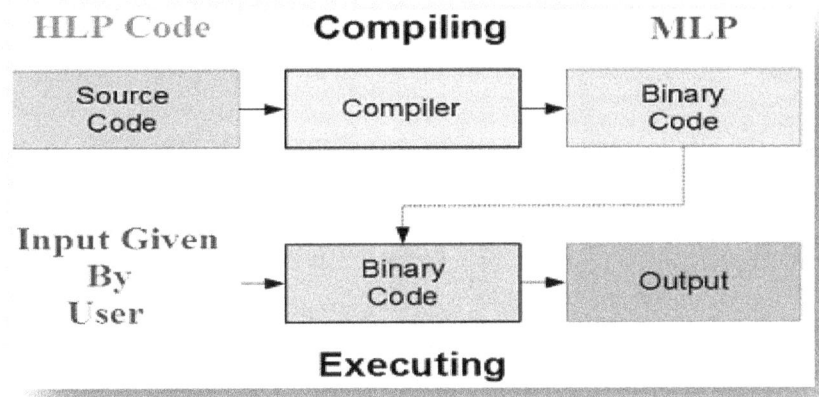

Fig. 2.3

Advantages

1. Source code is not included by compiler; therefore compiled code is more secure than interpreted code.

2. Compiler produces an executable file, and therefore the program can be run without need of the source code.

3. The object program can be used whenever required without the need to of recompilation.

Disadvantages

1. When an error is found, the whole program (Source Code) has to be re-compiled again & again.

2. Object code needs to be produced before a final executable file; this can be a slow process.

Interpreter

An **interpreter** is a translator program which translates statements of a program into machine code. It translates only one statement of the program (Source code) at a time. It reads only one statement of program at a time, translates it and executes it. Then it reads the next statement of the program again translates it and executes it. In this way it proceeds further till all the statements are translated and executed successfully.

On the other hand, a compiler translates entire program and then translates the entire program into machine codes. A compiler is 10 to 25 times faster than an interpreter .By the compiler; the machine codes are saved permanently for future reference. On the other hand, the machine codes produced by interpreter are not saved. An interpreter is a small program as compared to compiler. It occupies less memory space, so it can be used in a smaller system which has limited memory space.

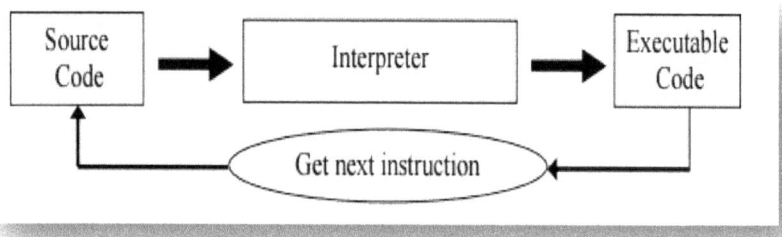

Fig. 2.4

Advantages

1. If an error is found then there is no need to retranslate the whole program like compiler.
2. Debugging (check errors) is easier since the interpreter stops when it finds an error.
3. Easier to create multi-platform (Run on different operating system) code, as each different platform would have an interpreter to run the same source code.

Disadvantages

1. Source code is required for the program to be executed, and this source code can be read by any other programmer so it is not a secured.

2. Interpreters are generally slower than compiled programs because interpreter translates one line at a time.

Difference between Compiler & Interpreter:

Compiler	Interpreter
Compiler Takes Entire program as input	Interpreter Takes Single instruction as input
Compiler generates object code	Interpreter is not generates object code
No source code is required in executable fie	Source code is required in executable file
It is secured	It is not Secured
Memory Requirement is large	Memory requirement is small
Errors are displayed after complete program is checked	Errors are displayed for every instruction interpreted (if any)
Debugging is Hard	Debugging is Easier
Programming language like C, C++,C# uses compilers.	Programming language like Python, Ruby uses interpreters.

2.3 Tokens In C

A **token** is the smallest individual element of a C program that is meaningful to the compiler. As we know that Software is a Program and a Program is that which Contains set of instructions, and an Instruction contains Some Tokens. The programmer can write a program by using tokens.

There are five types of tokens in C language:
1. Keywords
2. Variables/Identifiers
3. Constants/Literals
4. Punctuators

UNIT-II   Introduction To C Language

5. Operators

1. **Keywords:**

Keywords are a set of words which are used for special purposes while writing a program. They are also known as reserved words. Their meaning is predefined. We cannot use keywords as a variable name is program.

Some of the keywords are listed below in C:

auto	break	case	char
const	continue	default	do
double	else	enum	extern
float	for	goto	if
int	long	register	return
short	signed	sizeof	static
struct	switch	typedef	union
unsigned	void	volatile	while

Fig.2.5

2. **Variables/Identifiers**

A variable can be defined in many ways. At the basic level, a variable can be defined as a memory location declared to store any kind of data (which may change many times during program execution). It can also be defined as any entity which may vary during program execution. To identify a variable (the declared memory location), it can be assigned a name – known as variable name. ***The name given to a variable is known as an identifier.*** An identifier can be a combination of alphabets, digits and underscore. There are certain set of rules which must be observed while naming a variable.

In computer programming, We cannot use operands directly means in case if we want to add two numbers, then we cannot use directly **1+1 OR 5+6** like that. For achieve the objective we must use a variable instead direct values.

Rules for naming a variable:-

- A variable name can be any combination of alphabets, digits and underscore.

- First character should be a letter (alphabet).

- Length of variable name can range from 1 to 8. (**Note:** Different compilers may allow different ranges, say up to 31. But it is a good practice to keep the variable name short.)

- A space in between is not allowed. **Ex:** A variable name cannot be declared as **First Name.**

- Underscore can be used to concatenate name combinations. **Ex**: **First_Name** are valid identifiers.

- We cannot use commas or other special characters (other than underscore _) are allowed in a variable name.

- There are certain reserved words in C language, known as keywords. Words similar to a keyword cannot be used as a variable name. **Ex:** – In the previous article on data types, we saw **int**, **char,float** etc. These are actually keywords. So you can't declare a variable with names **int**, **char** or **float**.

While creating variable name in program here some are recommendations which programmer must follow-

- Variable Name must be start with capital letter.

For example: Age , Email , Phone

- If you have combinations of two words then Initials must be capital letter of words.

For example: FirstName , RollNo, LocalAdd

- Varicable name must be relate with proper identification. Don't use a variable name like a,b,c.

For example: Age , Name , Email , Mobile , PinCode , Sum , Total

Variable Declaration

A variable must be declared first before we can use it in a program for manipulations. A variable is declared with its storage class, data type (Explain in next sections) and identifier. The format is shown below:-

Storage-class   Data-Type   Variable-name;

Storage class is something which we will learn in coming chapters. By default all variable declarations (without any storage class specified) will be assigned to **"automatic storage class".** We will discuss more about storage class in another chapter.

So our variable declaration would be like:-

Data-Type   Variable-name;

Examples:-
>   int Age;
>   int Page;
>   char Name;

Two or more variables of the same data type can be declared in a single line, separating each variable name with a comma and ending the line with a semicolon.

Examples:-
>   int Age,Pages,Days;
>   char FirstName , LastName

Initial values can be assigned to variables while declaring it.

Examples:-
>   int Age=19 , Page=200;

Now we will see a situation where we have declare the variable

Int Age=19;

Here we have declared a variable of data **type integer** with **name as Age** and initial **value as 19.** This declaration tells the C compiler to:-

- Reserve space in memory to hold the integer value.
- Assign the name 'Age' to that reserved memory space.
- Store the value 19 in this memory location.

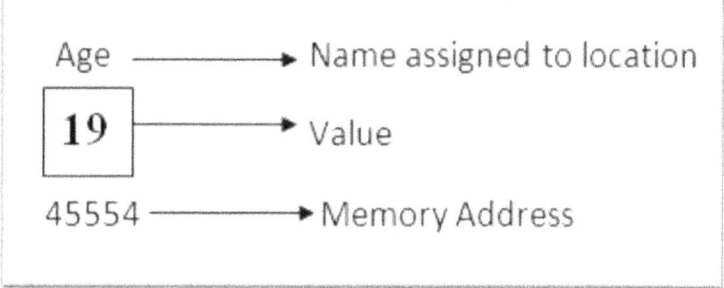

Fig. 2.5

3. Constants/Literals

The term constants or literals refer to the fixed value means a Constant is that whose value is never changed at the execution of program. The following types of literals are available in C.

1. Integer-Constants
2. Character-constants
3. Floating-constants
4. Strings-constants

UNIT-II   Introduction To C Language

1. Integer Literals

These are integers and they do not have any decimal/fractional part. It may contain either + or − sign, but decimal point or commas does not appear in any integer constant. C allows three types of integer constants.

- ✓ Decimal (Base 10)
- ✓ Octal (Base 8)
- ✓ Hexadecimal (Base 16)

- ✓ **Decimal integer constants** It consists of sequence of digits and should not begin with 0 (zero).

    For example: 174,145, - 178, + 109.

- ✓ **Octal integer constants** It consists of sequence of digits starting with 0 (zero).

    For example: 011, 012.

- ✓ **Hexadecimal integer constant** It consists of sequence of digits preceded by ox or OX.

    For example: OXD, OXC. The suffix l or L and u or U attached to any constant forces it to be represented as a long and unsigned respectively.

2. Character-constants

A character constant in C must contain one or more characters and must be enclosed in single quotation marks (' '). C allows characters which cannot be typed directly from keyboard, like backspace, tab, carriage return etc. These characters can be represented by using a escape sequence. An escape sequence represents a single character. The following table gives a listing of common escape sequences used in programming effectively

Escape Sequence	Character
\n	Newline or line feed

\t	Horizontal tab
\r	Carriage return
\v	Vertical tab
\?	Question mark
\"	Double quote
\'	Single quote

3. Floating Literals

These are numbers that have a decimal part. They are also called real constants. They are numbers having fractional parts. They may be written in fractional form or exponent form. They can be signed and unsigned.

While representing decimal form, you must include the decimal point, the exponent, or both; and while representing exponential form, you must include the integer part, the fractional part, or both. The signed exponent is introduced by e or E.

For Example: 127.32, -12.9 , 2E03, 1.23E07

4. String Literals

A sequence of character enclosed within double quotes is called a string literal. String literal is by default (automatically) added with a special character '\0' which denotes the end of the string. Therefore the size of the string is increased by one character.
For example: "COMPUTER" will be represented as "COMPUTER\0" in the memory and its size is 9 characters.

4. Punctuators

The following characters are used as punctuators in C.

Punctuator	Use	Example
< >	Header name	<stdio.h>
Brackets [ ]	Array Delimiter	Int a[5];
Parentheses ( )	Used in function arguments	Int fun(int x,int y);
Braces { }	Opening and closing braces indicate the start and end of a compound statement/function.	Main() { }
Comma ,	It is used as a separator in a function argument list, Variable list.	Int a,b,c;
Semicolon ;	It is used as a statement terminator/End of line.	Int Age;
Colon :	It indicates a labeled statement or conditional operator symbol.	A=1?20:30;
Asterisk *	Pointer declaration	Int *a;
Equal sign =	It is used as an assignment operator.	A=5; B=A;
Pound sign #	It is used as pre-processor directive.	#include #define
Double colon ::	Scope resolution operator for Identify same function with different class.	Class A::test()

5. Operators

An operator is a symbol which tells compiler to take an action on operands and evaluate a value. The Value on which operator operates is called as operands. C supports wide verity of operators. C provides six types of operators.

If c= (a + b) then + is operator & a, b, c are operands.

Operator	Explanation
Arithmetic Operators	Used for arithmetic operations
Relational Operators	Used for specifying relation between two operands
Logical Operators	Used for identifying the truth value of the expression
Bitwise Operators	Used for shifting the bits
Assignment Operators	Used for assigning the value to the variable
Misc Operators	

Arithmetic Operators

If the value of a=10 & b=5 then: –

Operator	Description	Example
+	Summation of two values	a + b=15
-	Substrate operands value	a-b=5
*	Multiply two operands value	a*b=50
/	Divide two operands value	a/b=2
%	After dividing the numerator by denominator value remainder will be returned after division	a % b=0

| ++ | Increment the value by one | a++=11 |
| -- | Decrement the value by one | a--=9 |

Relational Operators

Operator	Description	Example
>	Checks if the value of left operand is greater than the value of right operand, if yes then condition becomes true.	a is greater than b
<	Checks if the value of left operand is less than the value of right operand, if yes then condition becomes true.	b is less than a
<=	Checks if the value of left operand is less than or equal to the value of right operand, if yes then condition becomes true.	-----
>=	Checks if the value of left operand is greater than or equal to the value of right operand, if yes then condition becomes true.	-----
==	Checks if the values of two operands are equal or not, if yes then condition becomes true.	a & b not equals so condition false.
!=	Checks if the values of two operands are equal or not, if values are not equal then condition becomes true.	a & b is not equals so condition true.

Logical Operators

The logical operators are used to combine one or more relational expression. The following table shows the logical operators.

Operators	Meaning
&&	Logical AND & both conditions must be true
||	Logical OR & either conditions must be true
!	It is unary operators, it revert the value

Example:

    int x = 5; int z = 9;
    int y = 7;
    (x > y) & & (z > y)

The first expression (x > y) evaluates to false and second expression (z > y) evaluates to true. Therefore, the final expression is false.

✓ In AND operation, if any one of the expression is false, the entire expression is false.

✓ In OR operation, if any one of the expression is true, the entire expression is true.

✓ In NOT operation, only one expression is required. If the expression is true, the NOT operation of true is false and vice versa.

Bitwise Operators

There are used to change individual bits into a number. They work with only integral data types like char, int and long and not with floating point values

- ✓ Bitwise AND operators &
- ✓ Bitwise OR operator |
- ✓ And bitwise XOR operator ^
- ✓ And, bitwise NOT operator ~

UNIT-II Introduction To C Language

- ✓ Shift bits left <<
- ✓ Shift bits right >>

They can also be used with shorthand notation too:

&= , |= ,

^= , ~= etc.

Assignment Operator

Operates '=' is used for assignment, it takes the right-hand side and copy it into the left-hand side. Assignment operator is used in programming languages to copy one value of variable into other variable.

Example:

int a=5,b;

b=a;

On above value of 'a' which is 5 assign to variable b.

Example:

int a,b,c;

a=b=c=5

In addition to standard assignment operator shown above, C++ also supports compound assignment operators.

Misc. Operators

There are few other operators supported by C++ Language.

Operator	Description
sizeof	**sizeof operator** returns the size of a variable. For example, sizeof(a), where a is integer, will return 2.
Condition ? X : Y	**Conditional operator**. If Condition is true ? then it returns value X : otherwise value Y
Cast	**Casting operators** convert one data type to another. For example, int(5.25000) would return 5.
&	**Pointer operator &** returns the address of an variable. For example &a; will give actual address of the variable.

2.4 Data Types in C

Data types define the way you utilize storage (memory) in the programs that you write. By specifying a data type, you tell the compiler how to create a particular piece of storage, and also how to manipulate that storage. Data types & variables are interrelated because we have to use both in a single line in programming. Each & every variable must have some data types.

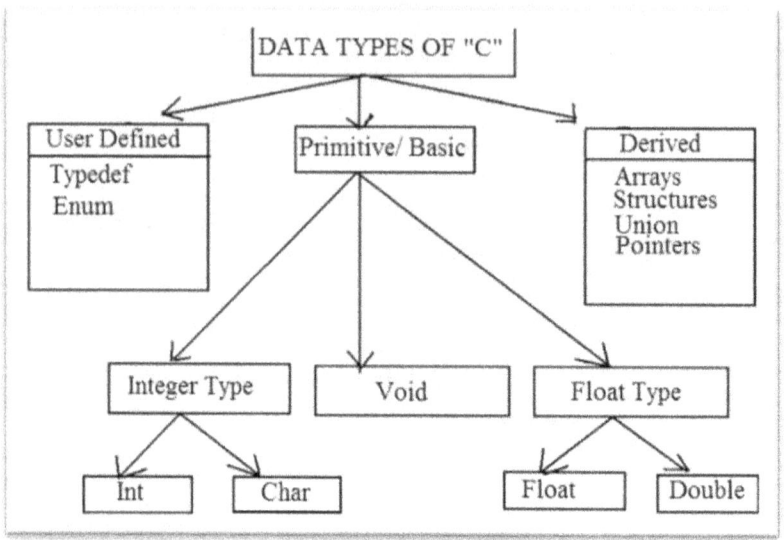

Fig. 2.6

Built-In Data Types

Built-in data types are basic or primitive data types. For each of the fundamental data types the range of values and the operations that can be performed on variables of that data type are determined by the compiler. Each compiler should provide the same operations for a particular data type but the range of values may vary between different compilers. There are 4 built-in data types in C++

- ✓ Int
- ✓ Float
- ✓ Char
- ✓ Double

Integer

Integer data type is used to store whole number. This data type does not contain any decimal portion. Integer data type occupied 2 Bytes in memory. If we want to calculate the age or number of pages then we must use integer data type.

Integer can be of two types:

- Signed Integer
- UnSigned Integer

Signed integers can hold positive or negative values, and unsigned integers can hold only positive values.

NOTE:
If your computer is an 8 bit computer then range of int is
$-2^{(8-1)} <$ integer number $< + [2^{(8-1)}] - 1$
$-128 <$ integer number $< +127$

The C programming languages allow the names of certain integer types to be abbreviated for integer variable definitions. For signed integer types, you can use the following abbreviations:

Full data type name	Abbreviated data type name
signed short int	short
signed int	int
signed long int	long
signed long long int	long long
unsigned short int	unsigned short
unsigned int	unsigned
unsigned long int	unsigned long
unsigned long long int	unsigned long long

Examples

int x = 2;
signed long y = 8;
long z;
unsigned int value;

UNIT-II   Introduction To C Language

unsigned long squarevalue;

value = 16;
squarevalue = value * value;

The following table shows the variable type, how much memory it takes to store the value in memory, and what is maximum and minimum value which can be stored in such type of variables.

Type	Size	Typical Range
int	2 or 4 bytes	-32,768 to 32,767 or -2,147,483,648 to 2,147,483,647
unsigned int	2 or 4 bytes	0 to 65,535 or 0 to 4,294,967,295
Short	2 bytes	-32,768 to 32,767
unsigned short	2 bytes	0 to 65,535
Long	4 bytes	-2,147,483,648 to 2,147,483,647
unsigned long	4 bytes	0 to 4,294,967,295

To get the exact size of a type or a variable on a particular platform, you can use the **size of** operator. The expressions *size of (type)* yields the storage size of the object or type in bytes.

Floating types

Variables of floating types can hold real values (numbers) such as: 7.134, -79.582 etc. Keywords either float or double is used for declaring floating type variable.

For example:
>float var1;
>double var2;

Here, both *var1* and *var2* are floating type variables.

Size and range of Integer type on 16-bit machine

Type	Size(bytes)	Range
Float	4	3.4E-38 to 3.4E+38
double	8	1.7E-308 to 1.7E+308
long double	10	3.4E-4932 to 1.1E+4932

Character types

Keyword char is used for declaring the variable of character type. For example:
char var1='h';

Here, *var1* is a variable of type character which is storing a character 'h'. The size of char is 1 byte.

Size and range of Integer type on 16-bit machine

Type	Size(bytes)	Range
char or signed char	1	-128 to 127
unsigned char	1	0 to 255

Void Type

Void type means no value. This is usually used to specify the type of functions. In C Programming we have most of the time used void main() because our main function does not return any values.

User Define Data Types

The C language allows you to create and use data types other than the fundamental data types. You can use UDTs to extend the built-in types already available and create your own customized data types. The C language provides you great flexibility on re-defining these existing types or re-defining new ones. These types are called user-defined data types. In C UDDT can be of four types:

- ✓ Structure
- ✓ Class
- ✓ Union
- ✓ Enumerations

(We will discussed all user define data types in next units.)

2.6 Expression & Statements

A combination of variables, constants and operators that represents a computation forms an expression. Depending upon the type of operands involved in an expression or the result obtained after evaluating expression, there are different categories of an expression. These categories of an expression are discussed here.

- ✓ **Integral expressions**
- ✓ **Float expressions**
- ✓ **Relational or Boolean expressions**
- ✓ **Logical expressions**
- ✓ **Bitwise expressions**
- ✓ **Pointer expressions**

Integral expressions

Integral expressions are those expressions which provide results in the form of integer values.

For example: x, 8*x-y, y+5 and 30 +int (15.0) are integral expressions.
Here, **x** and **y** are variables.

Float expressions

Float expressions are those expressions which provide results in the form of floating values.

For example: x, 8.5*x-y, y+5.5 and 30 +float (15) are integral expressions.
Here, **x** and **y** are variables.

Boolean expressions

The expressions that produce a bool type value, that is, either true or false are called **relational or Boolean expressions.**

For example: a+b>=10, a==b and a>=b+2 are integral expressions.
Here, **a** and **b** are variables.

Logical expressions

The expressions that produce a bool type value after combining two or more relational expressions are called **logical expressions.**

For example: (a>=18) && (a<=30) ,(a>=18) || (a<=30) are logical expressions.
Here, **a** and **b** are variables.

Bitwise expressions

The expressions which manipulate data at bit level are called **bitwise expressions.**

For example: a >> 14 and b<< 22 are bitwise expressions.
Here, **a** and **b** are variables.

Pointers expressions

UNIT-II Introduction To C Language

The expression which provides a address of any variable that is called pointers expressions.

For example: a=&b are pointers expressions.
Here, **a** and **b** are pointers variables.

2.7 Structure of C Program

As we know, every program language has its own syntax and we must follow all the syntax to make any program. Each program has predefined structure and we can create any program according to that structure. Like other programming language, C has its own structure for writing program.

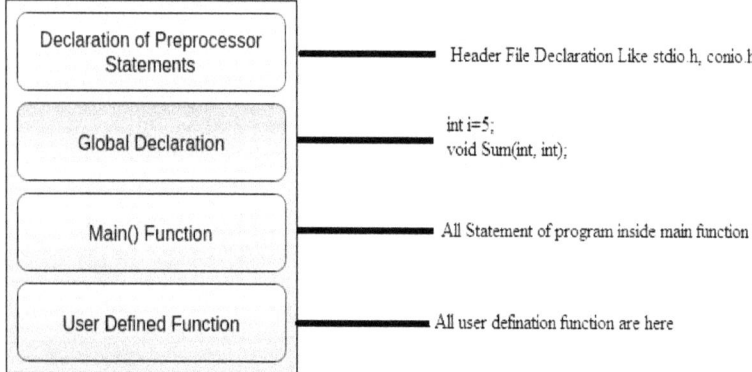

Fig.2.7

C program structure divided into following parts:

1. Declaration of Header file (Mandatory)
2. Global Declaration (Optional)
3. Main Function (Mandatory)
4. User Define function (Optional)

Declaration of Header file:

It is mandatory section of programming. Basically in this section, we can declare header file and as we know header file is collection of functions. If we are using any function then it is important for programmer to include header file in top of program else it will give you error.

For example, printf() & scanf() are output and input function, for this we must use standard input output header file (stdio.h).

Same as other header file we can use according to situation of program. Like clrscr() & getch() function uses console input output function (conio.h).

Declaration of Global Variable & Function Prototype:

In this section, if we have use any user defines function then we must define function prototype before main function. As same way, if we required any global variable (Global variable are those variable whose value is same for complete program and its scope throuout the program). It is not mandatory part of C program structure.

Declaration of Main Function:

It is the most important part of program. Every program has at least one function and that function is called main function. Without main function, we cannot create any program in C. Compilation process is always start from main function and also end with this function. All the statement declaration, loop statement, jumping statement is reside in this function.

User Define Function Definition:

All user define function definition is inside this section. It is only used when we have user define function in program. (Will discuss detail in unit IV)

UNIT - III

C BASIC PROGRAMMING & CONTROL STATEMENT

3.1 Basics of C

In any programming required output is important because every user wants to see output, but as a developer point of view it is highly important that the programmer must follow some coding standards. Coding standards/Guidelines are very important because if we write code in a proper format, use proper names of variables and the most important part is memory organization of any program. Coding standards are important for many reasons. First and foremost, they specify a common format for the source code and comments. This allows developers to easily share code, and the ideas expressed *within* the code and comments, between each other.

A coding standards document tells developers how they must write their code. Instead of each developer coding in their own preferred style, they will write all code to the standards guidelines in the document. This makes sure that a large program is coded in a proper style which very developers understand— parts are not written differently by different programmers. Not only does this solution make the code easier to understand, it also ensures that any developer who looks at the code will know what to expect throughout the entire application.

In this book we are giving some coding standards, It is not necessary to follow but for better programming it is highly recommended.

1. In the first line of the program, Use comment for declaring program description so any programmer understand that this is program for what purpose.

Examples:

/* This is program for addition of two number without using class*/

/* This is program for addition/multiplication of two number using switch*/

/*This is program for demonstration of multiple function*/

// This is an example of exception handling

What is Comment?

In computer programming, a **comment** is a programmer-readable statement in the source code of a computer program. They are added with the purpose of making the source code easier to understand, and are completely ignored by compilers and interpreters.

Comments can be of two types in C programming language.

A. **Single Line Comment**
B. **Multiline Comment**

A. <u>**Single Line Comment**</u> is used to comment out just Single Line in the Code. It is used to provide One Liner Description of line.

Some Important Points :

- ✓ Single Line Comment Can be **Placed Anywhere**
- ✓ Single Line Comment **Starts with '//'**
- ✓ Any Symbols written after '//' are **ignored by Compiler**
- ✓ Comment cannot hide statements written before '//' and On the Successive new line

For example:

/*
_____
_____ */

| UNIT-III | C Basic Programming & Control |
| Statement | |

B. <u>Multi Line Comment</u> is used for multiple lines in the Code. It is used to provide multi Liner Description of line.

Multi Line Comment

- ✓ Multi line comment can be placed anywhere.
- ✓ Multi line comment starts with /*.
- ✓ Multi line comment ends with */.
- ✓ Any symbols written between '/*' and '*/' are ignored by Compiler.
- ✓ It can be split over multiple lines

For example:

```
/*
_____
____
-------------------------------------------
---------
-------------------------------------------
-------*/
```

2. If any special header file used in program then we must mention the working of that header file in summarize way?

We will explain header file in the end of this chapter.

3. As we know very well that every function, loop & decision making statement start and end with curly braces so they must be in proper places for better understanding.

For example:

```
Void main()
    {
        ----------;
        ----------;
    }
```

```
------------
Void main ()
    {
        For ( ; ; )
            {
                If ( )
                    {
                        -------;
                        -------;
                    } // end of if
            } // end of for
    }   //enf of main
```

4. Variable name must be related with the purpose of declaration.

For example:

- ✓ If we want create a program for addition of two number then we have to use three variables so instead of using a,b,c we must provide proper variable name like :

    Int FNo,SNo,Total;

- ✓ First alphabets of variable name must be a capital letter.

    Int Multiplication;
    Float Per,Avg;

- ✓ If we use two words in variable name then first alphabet of every word must be capital letter.

    String FirstName;

UNIT-III Statement	C Basic Programming & Control

Int PrimeNumber;

5. When we use any user define function then it name must match with working of function and again it name start with capital latter.

For Example:

        int Sum (int x,int y);
        int PrimeNumber(int No);

3.2 Header File & Input/output Functions

Header file is collection of functions which must include in the program. A header file is a file with **extension .h** which contains C function declarations to be shared between several source files. Header file is also collection of codes, so writing that code again and again in every program is not a good idea. Instead of this, all the code declared inside header file and that header file is just including into the program. Including a header file produces the same results as copying the header file into each source file that needs it. Such copying would be time-consuming and error-prone. With a header file, the related declarations appear in only one place. If they need to be changed, they can be changed in one place, and programs that include the header file will automatically use the new version when next recompiled. The header file eliminates the labor of finding and changing all the copies as well as the risk that a failure to find one copy will result in inconsistencies within a program. **For example**, In C programming language we have used console input output header file (conio.h). This header file contains clrscr & getch functions. You request to use a header file in your program by including it with the C preprocessing directive **#include**.

The **#include** directive works by directing the preprocessor to scan the specified file as input before continuing with the rest of the current source file. The output from the preprocessor contains the output already generated, followed by the output resulting from the included file, followed by the output that comes from the text after the **#include** directive.

Syntax of include directive is:

#include <filename>
#include "filename "

Header files can be o two types:

- ✓ System defined header file
- ✓ User defined header file

System defined header file:

System defined header file are those file which is predefined and user cannot perform any changes. If you want to see the system defined header file in your system, then go inside the Include folder.

There are many headers file, below is the list of some header files:

No.	Name	Description
1	stdio.h	Input/output Functions
2	conio.h	console input/output
3	assert.h	Diagnostics Functions
4	ctype.h	Character Handling Functions
5	cocale.h	Localization Functions
6	math.h	Mathematics Functions
7	setjmp.h	Nonlocal Jump Functions

8	signal.h	Signal Handling Functions
9	stdarg.h	Variable Argument List Functions
10	stdlib.h	General Utility Functions
11	string.h	String Functions
12	time.h	Date and Time Functions

Some other header file lists are:

```
<algorithm>     <iomanip>      <list>       <queue>
<streambuf>
<bitset>        <ios>          <locale>     <set>
<string>
<complex>       <iosfwd>       <map>        <sstream>
<typeinfo>
<deque>         <iostream>     <memory>     <stack>
<utility>
<exception>     <istream>      <new>        <stdexcept>
<valarray>
<fstream>       <iterator>     <numeric>    <strstream>
<vector>
<functional>    <limits>       <ostream>
```

User Defined Header File

User define header file define by user according to own needs. As we already said that, header file is a collection of function so in user define header file user just writes function and use that file in program whenever it required.

(In next unit, we will create user define header file and used in our program as predefine header file used)

Input/ Output Function in C

Input means to provide the program with some data (Entered by the User) to be used in the program and **Output** means to display data on screen or write the data. For example, while using ATM machine, when screen display "Enter your pin" then it is called output and given by output function. In " " we can provide any value or string. When user entered pin number then it is called input and given by input function in programming.

C programming language provides many built-in functions to read any given input and to display data on screen when there is a need to output the result. All these built-in functions are present in C header files; we will also specify the name of header files in which a particular function is defined while discussing about it.

printf() function in c language:

- ✓ In C programming language, printf() function is used to print the "character, string, float, integer, octal and hexadecimal values" onto the output screen and also you want to show any message or any instruction, for this you can also use printf() function.

- ✓ We use printf() function with %d format specifier to display the value of an integer variable.
- ✓ Similarly %c is used to display character, %f for float variable, %s for string variable, %lf for double and %x for hexadecimal variable.
- ✓ To generate a newline, we use "\n" in C printf() statement.

UNIT-III
C Basic Programming & Control Statement

Note:
> C language is case sensitive. For example, printf() and scanf() are different from Printf() and Scanf().

Examples:
> Printf("Enter the Value of A=");
> Printf("Enter the First value=");
> Printf("Enter the Value of A ::");
> Printf(" A ::::");
> Printf("Please enter value of A");

When we have used any formula or variable, and want to print on console screen, then we must use following way in printf():

> Printf(" %d", c);
> Printf("Sum of two number is= %d", c);
> Printf("%d + %d = %d", a, b, c);

Note: In C programming, semicolon (;) is statement terminator and it must be come after end of statement else compiler will give error.

scanf() function in c language:

- ✓ In C programming language, scanf() function is used to take input from the keyboard. Any input must be provided by this function and it has specific format and we must follow that format. Unlike in printf, we can use our own string or values in "" but in this scanf, we must follow specific syntax.

    First part of scanf consists of format specifier:

Format String	Meaning
%d	Scan or print an integer as signed decimal number
%f	Scan or print a floating point number
%c	To scan or print a character
%s	To scan or print a character string. The scanning ends at whitespace.

There are other input and output functions, which can be used in specific type and will discuss in next units.

3.3 First Program in C

Prog 3.1:: Write a simple program to demonstrate first C program.

```c
/* Program for addition of two number*/
#include<stdio.h>              // Header file
#include<conio.h>
void main()
{
    int FNo,SNo,Total;
    clrscr();                   // For clear the previous output
    printf("Enter the first Value::");
    scanf("%d",&FNo);           // Get first value from keyboard
    printf("Enter the Second Value::");
    scanf("%d",&SNo);           // Get second value from keyboard
    Total=FNo+SNo;
    printf(" Sum of two number is :: %d", Total);
    getch()                     // For holding the output screen on console
}
```

UNIT-III
Statement

C Basic Programming & Control

OUTPUT

```
Enter the first value:: 5
Enter the second value::6
Sum of two number is :: 11
```

In the above program, we have used stdio.h header file. stdio.h is known as standard input output header file which is used for input & output functions. In C, printf is an output function and it is used when we want to show output or any message on the screen. scanf is an input function, which takes value from the users.

clrscr & getch function is used to clear the previous output on the screen and hold the screen. Our program return a no value, so we have void main () instead of int main.

Compilation & Execution

When you write a C program, the next step is to compile the program before running it. The compilation is the processes which convert the program written in human readable language like C, C++ etc into a machine code, directly understood by the Central Processing Unit. There are many stages involved in creating a executable file from the source file. The stages include Preprocessing, Compiling and Linking in C. There are many C compilers around

Preprocessing

In this phase the preprocessor changes the code according to the directives mentioned (that starts with # sign). The C preprocessor takes the program and deals with the # include directives and the resulting program is pure C program. For example, in C program #include<stdio.h> will tell the preprocessor to read all the contents of the stdio header file and include/Use the contents into the program and generate the separate C program file. C supports many preprocessor directives like #include, #define, #if, #else etc.

Compilation

This step translates the source program into a assembly level code. The compiler takes the preprocessed file and generates an object file containing assembly level code. Compilation process looks like this:

1. The C preprocessor copies the contents of the included header files into the source code file, generates macro code, and replaces symbolic constants defined using #define with their values.
2. The expanded source code file produced by the C preprocessor is compiled into the assembly language for the platform.
3. The assembler code generated by the compiler is assembled into the object code for the platform.
4. The object code file generated by the assembler is linked together with the object code files for any library functions used to produce an executable file.

Linking

Linking as the name suggests, refers to creation of a single executable file from multiple object files. The file created after linking is ready to be loaded into memory and executed by the system. There is difference in linking and compilation when it comes to understanding errors. Compiler shows errors in syntax, for example semi-colon not mentioned, data type not defined etc but if there is an error that function has been defined multiple times, then this error is from linker as it's indicating that two or more source code files have the same meaning and that is leading to an error.

You might ask why there are separate compilation and linking steps. First, it's probably easier to implement things that way. The compiler does its thing, and the linker does its thing, by keeping the functions separate, the complexity of the program is reduced. Another advantage is that this allows the creation of large programs without having to redo the compilation step every time a file is changed. Instead, using so called "conditional compilation", it is necessary to compile only those source files that have changed; for the rest, the object files are sufficient input for the linker. Finally, this makes it simple to implement libraries of pre-compiled code: just create object files and link them just like any other object file.

Formatting Output

In every programming language, output is most important. For providing the required output programmer creates logic and implements that logic into any programming language, but formatting an output is also an important part of the program. Proper formatting style will give an easily understandable application; if another user used the output, then user understands that this output is for what purpose.

For example: On the above first program, the output is "Sum of two numbers is: __". Suppose we have not used this output style, then it does not affect on the program, but it is not user friendly output. On the same program for taking values from the user we can also write:

scanf("%d %d",&a, &b);

But this statement will give below output:

```
5 6
```

Now only the programmer can understand that this is a program for sum and we must provide values of a & b variables, but any other cannot understand easily, so for that purpose on above program we have written "Enter the value of A:" and "Enter the value of B:"

Examples:

```
5 + 6 = 11
```

For above output, we can write below statement:

c = a+b;
printf("%d + %d = %d",a,b,c);

```
Factorial of 5 is = 120
```

For above output, we can write below statement:

printf("Factorial of %d is = %d", N, Fact);

```
******************************
1. Addition
2. Multiplication
3. Subtraction
******************************
```

For above output, we can write below statement:

printf("******************************* \n");**
printf("1. Addition \n");
printf("2. Multiplication \n)";
printf("3. Subtraction \n)";
printf("******************************* \n");**

```
4 * 1 = 4
4 * 2 = 8
4 * 3 = 12
4 * 4 = 16
4 * 5 = 20
4 * 6 = 24
4 * 7 = 28
4 * 8 = 32
4 * 9 = 36
4 * 10 = 40
```

For above output, we can write below statement:

for (int i=1 ;i<=10;i++)
   {
   Mul= N * i ;
   printf("%d * %d = %d",N ,i,Mul);
   printf("\n");
   }

Prog 3.2:: Write a program to calculate the average of three numbers.

                /* Program for average of three numbers*/

#include<stdio.h>

#include<conio.h>

void main()

   {

   float a,b,c,d;

| UNIT-III | C Basic Programming & Control |
| Statement | |

```
clrscr();
printf("Enter the first Value::");
scanf("%f",&a);
printf("Enter the Second Value::");
scanf("%f",&b);
printf("Enter the Third Value::");
scanf("%f",&c);
d=(a+b+c) / 3;
printf(" Average of three number is :: %f", d);
getch()
}
```

OUTPUT

```
Enter the first value:: 5.2
Enter the second value:: 6.6
Enter the Third value:: 3.2
Average of three number is :: 3.0000
```

Prog 3.3:: Write a program to calculate the square of given numbers.

```
             /* Program for square of given numbers*/
#include<stdio.h>
#include<conio.h>
void main()
    {
    int a,n;
    clrscr();
    printf("Enter the Value of Square Number::");
    scanf("%d",&a);
    a= n * n ;
```

```
printf(" Square of % is :: %d", n, a);
getch()
}
```

OUTPUT

```
Enter the Value of Square Number:: 4
Square of 4 is :: 16
```

Swapping Program

Swapping of two numbers is interchanging the values of two variables. For example, value of **a=5 and b=8** then after swapping program now value becomes **a=8 and b=5.**

Prog 3.4:: Write a program for swapping of two number using third variable.

UNIT-III Statement

C Basic Programming & Control

/* Program for Swapping */

```c
#include<stdio.h>
#include<conio.h>
void main()
{
    int a,b,c;
    clrscr();
    printf("Enter the Value of A::");
    scanf("%d",&a);
    printf("Enter the Value of B::");
    scanf("%d",&b);
    printf(" Before Swapping :: A = %d and B = %d", a,b)
    c= a;
    a= b;
    b= c;
    printf(" After Swapping :: A = %d and B = %d", a,b)
    getch()
}
```

OUTPUT

```
Enter the Value of A :: 4
Enter the Value of B :: 9
Before Swapping:: A = 4 and B = 9
After Swapping:: A = 9 and B = 4
```

In above logic, we have assign the first value into third variable and after that value of b assign the value of a.

c = 4

a = 9

b= 4

Prog 3.5:: Write a program for swapping of two number without using third variable.

```
/* Program for Swapping */
#include<stdio.h>
#include<conio.h>
void main()
   {
   int a,b;
   clrscr();
   printf("Enter the Value of A::");
   scanf("%d",&a);
   printf("Enter the Value of B::");
   scanf("%d",&b);
   printf(" Before Swapping :: A = %d and B = %d", a,b)
    a= a - b;
    b = a + b;
    a = b – a;
   printf(" After Swapping :: A = %d and B = %d", a,b)
   getch()
   }
```

UNIT-III C Basic Programming & Control
Statement

OUTPUT

Enter the Value of A :: 4
Enter the Value of B :: 9
Before Swapping:: A = 4 and B = 9
After Swapping:: A = 9 and B = 4

Explanation:

a = a – b   :   a = 4 – 9   :   a = -5

b = a + b   :   b = -5 + 9   :   b = 4

a = b – a;   a = 4 – (-5) :   a = 4+ 5   : a = 9

3.4 Control Statements

Control statements enable us to specify the flow of program control; i.e., the order in which the instructions in a program must be executed. They make it possible to make decisions, to perform tasks repeatedly or to jump from one section of code to another. To implements these "control structures" in a C/C++ program, the language provides 'control statements'. So to implement a particular control structure in a programming language, we need to learn how to use the relevant control statements in that particular language.

There are four types of control statements in C:

1. *Decision making/ Conditional statements/ Branching*
2. *Selection statements (Switch)*
3. *Iteration/ Loop statements*
4. *Jump statements*

Decision making/ Conditional statements/ Branching

Decision making or Conditional statement is about deciding the order of execution of statements based on certain conditions or repeat a group of statements until certain specified conditions are met. Decision making/Conditional statements require that the programmer will provide one or more conditions to be evaluated or tested by the program, along with a set of statement or statements to be executed if the condition is determined to be true, and optionally, other statements to be executed if the condition is determined to be false. The different forms are,

- ✓ Simple *if* statement
- ✓ *If....else* statement
- ✓ Nested *if....else* statement

Simple If Statement:

An **if statement** consists of a Boolean expression (Either it could be true or false) followed by one or more statements.

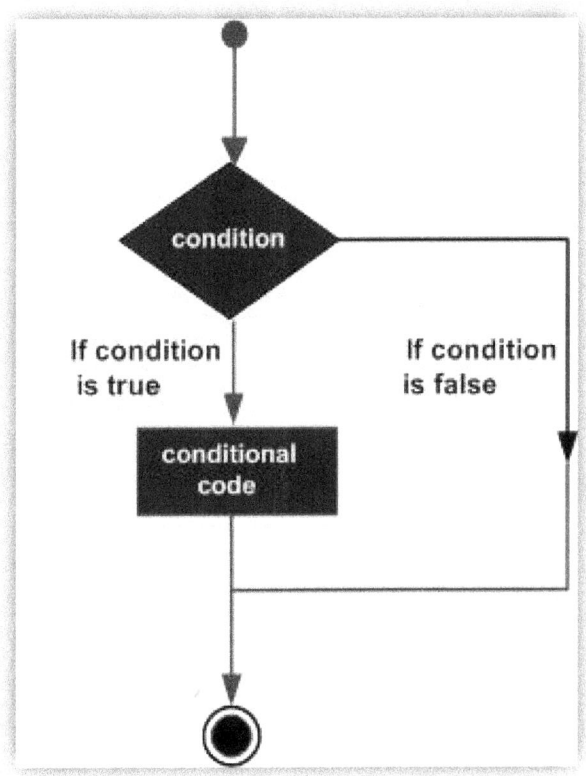

Fig.3.1

UNIT-III
Statement

Syntax:

If (expression)

  {

    Statement inside;

  }

  Statement outside;

Prog# 3.6: Write a Program to demonstrate the example of simple if statement.

```
                /* Program for Simple If statement */
#include<stdio.h>
#include<conio.h>
void main()
   {
    int No;
    clrscr();
    printf("Enter the Value of No::");
    scanf("%d",&No);
    if (No > 6)
      {
       printf(" Number is greater than 6.....");
      }
    getch()
   }
```

OUTPUT

```
Enter the Value of No :: 98
Number is greater than 6.....
```

If....Else Statements:

The if...else statement executes some code if the test expression is true (nonzero) and some other code if the test expression is false (0).

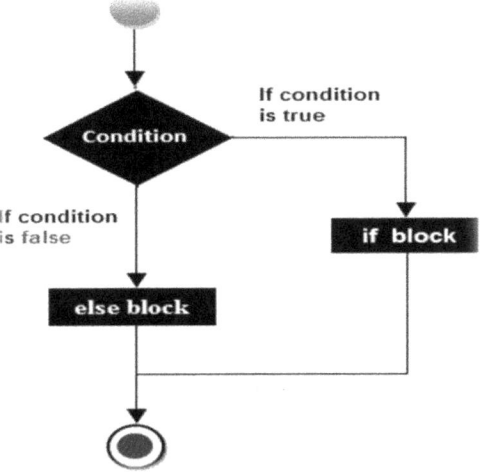

Fig. 3.2

Syntax:

if(expression)
  {
   Statement block1;
  }
else
  {
   Statement block2;
  }

UNIT-III C Basic Programming & Control Statement

If test expression is true, code inside the body of if statement is executed; and code inside the body of else statement is skipped. If test expression is false, code inside the body of else statement is executed; and code inside the body of if statement is skipped.

Prog# 3.7: **Write a Program to check whether the number is even or odd.**

/*Program to check whether the number is even or odd*/

```
#include<stdio.h>
#include<conio.h>
void main()
   {
    int No;
    clrscr();
    printf("Enter the Value of No::");
    scanf("%d",&No);
    if (No % 2 ==0)
       {
        printf (" Number is Even…..");
       }
    else
       {
        printf(" Number is odd…..");
       }
    getch()
   }
```

OUTPUT

```
Enter the Value of No :: 7
Number is odd......
```

When user enters 7, the test expression (No % 2 == 0) is evaluated to false. Hence, the statement inside the body of else statement is executed and the statement inside the body of if is skipped. In programming language, double equals (==) used when we want to compare two values.

Prog# 3.8: **Write a Program to check greatest of two numbers.**

```c
                /*Check greatest of two number*/
#include<stdio.h>
#include<conio.h>
void main()
  {
  int FNo , SNo;
  clrscr();
  printf("Enter the Value of First No::");
  scanf("%d",&FNo);
  printf("Enter the Value of Second No::");
  scanf("%d",&FNo);
  if ( FNo > SNo)
     {
     printf (" First Number is Greatest.....");
     }
  else
     {
     printf (" Second Number is Greatest.....");
     }
  getch()
  }
```

UNIT-III
Statement
C Basic PROGRAMMING & Control

```
Enter the Value of First No:: 7
Enter the Value of Second No:: 9
Second Number is Greatest .......
```

Prog# 3.9: **Write a Program to check whether the number is divisible by 7 or not.**

/*Program to check whether the number is divisible by 7 or not*/

```c
#include<stdio.h>
#include<conio.h>
void main()
   {
   int No;
   clrscr();
   printf("Enter the Value of No::");
   scanf("%d",&No);
   if (No % 7 ==0)
      {
      printf (" Number is Divisible by 7…..");
      }
   else
     {
     printf(" Number is Not Divisible by 7…..");
     }
   getch()
   }
```

68

OUTPUT

```
Enter the Value of No :: 81
Number is Not Divisible by 7……
```

Prog# 3.10: Write a Program to check whether the number is divisible by 4 and 9 .

/*Program to check whether the number is divisible by 4 and 9*/

```c
#include<stdio.h>
#include<conio.h>
void main()
  {
    int No;
    clrscr();
    printf("Enter the Value of No::");
    scanf("%d",&No);
    if ((No % 4 ==0) && (No % 9 ==0))
       {
         printf (" Number is Divisible by 4 and 9…..");
       }
    else
       {
         printf(" Number is Not Divisible by 4 and 9…..");
       }
    getch()
  }
```

UNIT-III
Statement   C Basic Programming & Control

OUTPUT

```
Enter the Value of No :: 36
Number is Divisible by 4 and 9......
```

Nested *if....else* statement:

It is also possible to nest if-else statements one within the other. Nesting is useful in situations where one of several different courses of action need to be selected. If one condition is false then second condition is tested, if second condition is false then third condition is tested and so on.

Syntax:

```
if(expression 1)    // Expression 1 is evaluated. If TRUE, statements inside the curly braces are executed.
{                               //If FALSE program control is
transferred to immediate else if statement.
statement 1;
statement 2;
}
else if(expression 2)   // If expression 1 is FALSE, expression 2 is evaluated.
{
statement 1;
statement 2;
}
else if(expression 3)   // If expression 2 is FALSE, expression 3 is evaluated
{
statement 1;
statement 2;
}
/* If all expressions (1, 2 and 3) are FALSE, the
statements that follow this else (inside curly
braces) is executed.*/
else
{
statement 1;
statement 2;
}
other statements;
```

The above is also called the **if-else ladder**. During the execution of a nested if-else statement, as soon as a condition is encountered which evaluates to true, the statements associated with that particular if-block will be executed and the remainder of the nested if-else statements will be bypassed. If neither of the conditions are true, either the last else-block is executed or if the else-block is absent, the control gets transferred to the next instruction present immediately after the else-if ladder.

Prog# 3.11: Write a Program to check greatest among three numbers.

```
                /*Check greatest among three numbers*/
#include<stdio.h>
#include<conio.h>
void main()
   {
   int FNo , SNo, TNo;
   clrscr();
   printf("Enter the Value of First No::");
   scanf("%d",&FNo);
   printf("Enter the Value of Second No::");
   scanf("%d",&FNo);
   printf("Enter the Value of Third No::");
   scanf("%d",&TNo);

   if ( (FNo > SNo) && (FNo > TNo))
      {
      printf(" First Number is Greatest.....");
      }
   else if ( (SNo > FNo) && (SNo > TNo))
         {
          printf(" Second Number is Greatest.....");
         }
   else
      {
      printf(" Third Number is Greatest.....");
      }
   getch()
   }
```

OUTPUT

```
Enter the Value of First No:: 7
Enter the Value of Second No:: 9
Enter the Value of Second No:: 6
Second Number is Greatest.......
```

Jumping Statement

There are some situations in programming where we want to transfer the program control from one place to another; jumping statement are set of keywords which are responsible to transfer program's control within the same block or from one function to another.

There are four jumping statements in C language:

- ✓ Break statement
- ✓ Continue statement
- ✓ Goto statement
- ✓ Return statement

Break Statement

Break is used with looping statement and switch statements, when compiler finds the break statement inside a loop, compiler will terminate the loop and continue to execute statements followed by loop.

Prog# 3.11: **Write a Program to Demonstrate the Example of Break.**

```c
/*Break Statement Example*/
#include<stdio.h>
#include<conio.h>
void main()
    {
    int i;
    clrscr();
    for( i=1;i<=5;i++)
        {
        if ( i = = 3 )
            {
            break;
            }
        printf("%d", i);
        }
    printf("\nTermination of loop.");
    getch()
    }
```

OUTPUT

```
12
Termination of loop.
```

Continue Statement

The continue statement is also used inside loop. Whenever it is encountered inside a loop, control directly jumps to the beginning of the loop for next iteration, skipping the execution of statements inside loop's body for the current iteration.

UNIT-III Statement C Basic Programming & Control

Prog# 3.12: Write a Program to Demonstrate the Example of Continue.

```
                    /*Continue Statement Example*/
#include<stdio.h>
#include<conio.h>
void main()
   {
    int i;
    clrscr();
    for( i=1;i<=5;i++)
       {
        if ( i = = 3 )
           {
            continue;
           }
        printf("%d", i);
       }
    printf("\nTermination of loop.");
    getch()
   }
```

OUTPUT

```
1 2 4 5
Termination of loop.
```

Value 3 is missing in the output, why? When the value of variable i is 3, the program encountered a continue statement, which makes the control to jump at the beginning of the for loop for next iteration, skipping the statements for current iteration (that's the reason printf didn't execute when i is equal to 3).

GOTO Statement

When there are some situations, where we want to change the flow of program then we have to use GOTO statement. A goto statement in C programming provides an unconditional jump from the 'goto' to a labeled statement in the same function. In programming, this concept is not used by programmers and for programmer point of view it is not a good concept for implementation.

Syntax

The syntax for a **goto** statement in C is as follows −

```
goto label;
..
.
label: statement;
```

Prog# 3.13: Write a Program to Demonstrate the Example of GOTO.

```
#include<stdio.h>
void main()
    {
      printf("\nStatement 1.");
      printf("\nStatement 2.");
      printf("\nStatement 3.");

      goto last;
      printf("\nStatement 4.");
      printf("\nStatement 5.");
      last:
            printf("\nEnd of Program.");
    }
```

UNIT-III
Statement

C Basic Programming & Control

OUTPUT

Statement 1.
Statement 2.
Statement 3.

End of Program

Loop Statement

Loops are very basic and very useful programming facility that facilitates programmer to execute any block of code lines repeatedly and can be controlled as per conditions added by programmer. It saves writing code several times for same task.

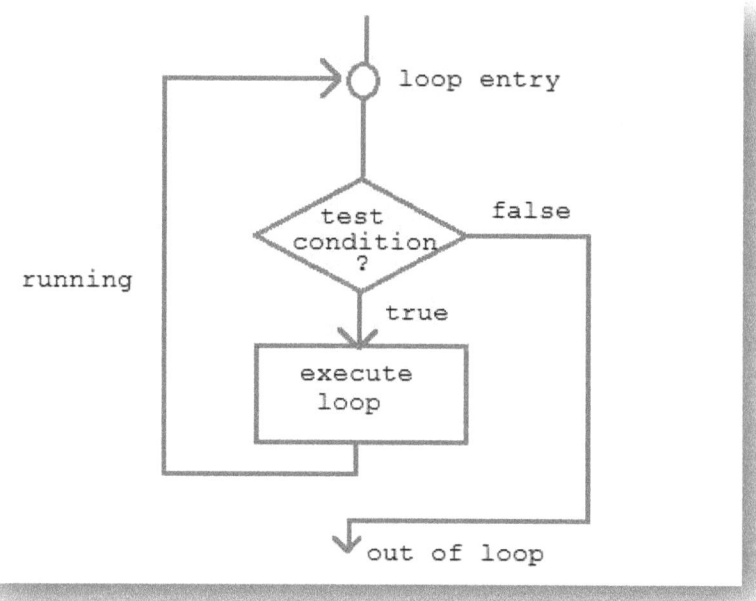

Fig. 3.3

A Sequence of statements is executed until a specified condition is met. This sequence of statements to be executed is kept inside the curly braces { } known as the **Loop body**. After every execution of loop body, condition is verified, and if it is found to be **true** the loop body is executed again. When the condition check returns **false**, the loop body is not executed.

There are 3 types of loop –

- ✓ While loop
- ✓ Do….while loop
- ✓ For loop

While Loop

While loop repeats a statement or group of statements while a given condition is true. It tests the condition before executing the loop body.

Basic syntax to use 'while' loop is:

Variable initialization;

While (condition to control loop)

   {

      statement 1;

      statement 2;

    ..

    ..

      iteration of variable;

   }

- **Variable initialization** is the initialization of variable of loop before start of 'while' loop, for example when we want to start our loop from 10 than we have to initialize our variable like:

i=10;

- **Condition** is any logical condition that controls the number of times execution of loop statements, for example while writing

UNIT-III
Statement

multiplication table, we know that it will start from 1 and ends with 10 so here condition is:

$$i<=10 \text{ (If I =1)}$$

- **Iteration** is the increment/decrement of counter, for example, when we take above example then value of I is increment in each iteration so

$$i ++ ;$$

Prog# 3.13: Write a Program for counting (1 to 10) using while loop.

```c
#include <stdio.h>
#include <conio.h>
void main()
   {
    int count=1;
    clrscr();
    while (count <= 10)
       {
           printf("%d ", count);
           count++;
       }
    getch();
   }
```

OUTPUT

12345678910

Prog# 3.14: Write a program to reverse the digits using 'While' loop.

/*Program to print reverse of digits using while loop*/

```
#include <stdio.h>
#include <conio.h>
void main()
    {
    int No,Rev;
    clrscr();
    printf(" Enter the Number: ");
    scanf("%d", &No);
    Rev=0;
    while (No !=0)
            {
            Rev = Rev * 10;
            Rev = Rev + No %10;
            No = No /10;
            }
    printf("\n Reverse of digits is: %d",Rev);
    getch();
    }
```

OUTPUT

Enter the Number: 5694

Reverse of digits is :4965

Explanation:

No = 5694
Rev = 0

Rev = Rev * 10;
Rev = Rev + No %10;
No = No /10;

    I.   **Rev = 0**

| | Rev=0+5694%10 = 0+4 | = 4 |
| | No= 569 | |

II. No = 569
     Rev=4

     Rev=40
     Rev=40+569%10 = 40+ 9   =49
     No = 56

III. No = 56
     Rev=49

     Rev=49+56%10 = 49+ 6   =496
     No= 5

IV. No = 5
     Rev=496

     Rev=496
     Rev=496+5% 10 = 496+5   =4965

Prog# 3.15: Write a program to check whether the number is palindrome or not.

/*Program to check palindrome*/

```
#include <stdio.h>
#include <conio.h>
void main()
    {
    int No,Rev,temp;
    clrscr();
    printf(" Enter the Number: ");
    scanf("%d", &No);
    Rev=0;
    Temp=No;
    while (No !=0)
        {
        Rev = Rev * 10;
```

```
          Rev = Rev + No %10;
          No = No /10;
              }
    if ( temp==Rev)
        printf("\n Digits is palindrome...") ;
    else
        printf("\n Digits is not palindrome...");;
    getch();
    }
```

OUTPUT

Enter the Number: 6996

Digit is palindrome...

Do.... While Loop

In do while loop body of the loop is always executed first. Then, the test condition is evaluated. If the test condition is TRUE, the program executes the body of the loop again. If the test condition is FALSE, the loop terminates and program execution continues with the statement following the while.

Syntax:
```
do
  {
   statement/s;
  } while (test expression);
```

In do...while loop, the body of loop is executed at least once.

Prog# 3.16: Write a program to demonstrate the example of 'do..While' loop.

```
            /*Program to print 1 To 10 using while loop*/
#include <stdio.h>
#include <conio.h>
void main()
    {
```

UNIT-III
Statement

```
    int count=1;
    clrscr();
    do
       {
          printf("%d ", count);
          count++;
       } while (count <=10);
    getch();
}
```

OUTPUT

12345678910

For Loop:

The statements in the for loop repeat continuously for a specific number of times. The for loop repeats until a specific count is met. For loop can be used when the number of repetition is know, or can be supplied by the user. The coding format is:

for (initialization; condition; increase)
   {
      block of code;
   }

It works in the following way:

- ✓ Initialization is executed. Generally, this declares a counter variable, and sets it to some initial value. This is executed a single time, at the beginning of the loop.
- ✓ Condition is checked. If it is true, the loop continues; otherwise, the loop ends, and statement is skipped, going directly to step 5.
- ✓ Statement is executed. As usual, it can be either a single statement or a block enclosed in curly braces { }.
- ✓ Increase is executed, and the loop gets back to step 2.
- ✓ The loop ends: execution continues by the next statement after it.

Look at the example below:

```
#include<stdio.h >
void main()
    {
      int i;
      for (i = 0; i < 10; i++)
          {
          printf( "Hello\n");
          printf("There\n");
          }

    }
```

Lets look at the "for loop" from the example: We first start by setting the variable i to 0. This is where we start to count. Then we say that the for loop must run if the counter i is less than 10. Last we say that every cycle i must be increased by one (i++).

In the example we used i++ which is the same as using i = i + 1. This is called incrementing. The instruction i++ adds 1 to i. If you want to subtract 1 from i you can use i–. It is also possible to use ++i or -i. The difference is is that with ++i the one is added before the "for loop" tests if i < 10. With i++ the one is added after the test i < 10.

Prog# 3.17: **Write a program for multiplication table of any given number.**

/*Program to print multiplication table*/

```
#include <stdio.h>
#include <conio.h>
void main()
    {
    int No,I , Mul;
    clrscr();
    printf(" Enter the Number: ");
    scanf("%d", &No);
    for(I=1;I<=10;I++)
```

UNIT-III
C Basic Programming & Control Statement

```
        {
        Mul= No*I;
        printf(" %d * %d  = %d", No, I, Mul);
        }
    getch();
    }
```

OUTPUT

```
Enter the No : 6

6 * 1 =6
6 * 2 =12
6 * 3 =18
6 * 4 =24
6 * 5 =30
6 * 6 =36
6 * 7 =42
6 * 8 =48
6 * 9 =54
6 * 10 =60
```

Prog# 3.18: **Write a program to find factorial of any given number.**

```
            /*Program to find factorial of a given number*/
#include <stdio.h>
#include <conio.h>
void main()
    {
    int No,I , Fact=1;
    clrscr();
    printf(" Enter the Number: ");
    scanf("%d", &No);
    for(I=1;I<=No;I++)
        {
        Fact= Fact * I;
        }
     printf(" Factorial of Given No is = %d", Fact);
    getch();
    }
```

OUTPUT

```
Enter the Number : 5
Factorial of a given number is :120
```

Prog# 3.19: Write a program to find whether the number is prime or not.

```c
/* Program to find 'Is number is prime or not' */
#include <stdio.h>
#include <conio.h>
void main()
    {
    int No,I ;
    clrscr();
    printf(" Enter the Number: ");
    scanf("%d", &No);
    for(I=2;I<=No-1;I++)
            {
            if(No% I ==0)
                    {
                    printf("\n Number is not prime..");
                    break;
                    }
            }
    if(No ==i)
            printf("\n No is prime..");
    getch();
    }
```

OUTPUT

```
Enter the Number : 7

No is prime..
```

UNIT-III
C Basic Programming & Control Statement

Prog# 3.20: **Write a program to print half pyramid using ' * '.**

```c
/* Program to print half pyramid */
#include <stdio.h>
#include <conio.h>
void main()
    {
    int I,j ;
    clrscr();
    for(I=1;I<=5;++I)
        {
        for(j=1;j<=i;++j)
            {
            printf(" * ");
            }
        printf("\n");
        }
    getch();
    }
```

OUTPUT

```
*
* *
* * *
* * * *
* * * * *
```

Prog# 3.21: **Write a program to print half pyramid using number.**

```c
/* Program to print half pyramid using number */
#include <stdio.h>
#include <conio.h>
void main()
    {
    int I,j ;
    clrscr();
    for(I=1;I<=5;++I)
```

```
        {
    for(j=1;j<=i;++j)
        {
        printf(" %d ", I);
        }
        printf("\n");
    }
  getch();
}
```

OUTPUT

```
1
1 1
1 1 1
1 1 1 1
1 1 1 1 1
```

3.5 Comparision Of For, While, Do..While Loop

- ✓ In for loop, initialization, condition and statements are all put together in one line which makes loop easier to understand and implement. While in the while loop, initialization is done prior to the beginning of the loop. Conditional statement is always put at the start of the loop. While adjustment can be either combined with condition or embedded into the body of the loop.

- ✓ When using "continue;" statement in for loop, control transfers to statement while in while loop control transfers to the condition statement.

- ✓ Both for and while loops are entry controlled loops that means test condition is checked for truth while entering into the loop's body.

- ✓ The for loop seems most appropriate when number of iteration are known in advance, for example, counting array elements. But, there could be many complex problems where number of iterations depend

UNIT-III
Statement

upon a certain condition and can't be predicated beforehand, in those situation programmers usually prefer to use while loop.

- ✓ **Do while** loop will be executed at least once but **while** loop will check the condition first and then it may or may not get executed depending on the condition.

- ✓ While is a entry -controlled loop but do-while is an exit-controlled loop.

- ✓ In while, condition comes before the body, but in do-while, condition comes after the body.

For loop	While loop	Do....while loop
for(n = 1; n <= 10; n++) { ======== ======== }	n = 1; while(n <=10) { ======== ======== n=n+1; }	n = 1; do { ======== ======== n = n + 1; } while(n<=10);

Selection Statement / Switch Statement

Switch statement is used to solve multiple option type problems for menu like program, where one value is associated with each option. The nested if...else statement allows you to execute a block code among many alternatives. If you are checking on the value of a single variable in <u>nested if...else statement</u>, it is better to use switch statement. The switch statement is often faster than nested if...else (not always).

Syntax:

```
switch(expression)
{
case value-1:
        block-1;
        break;
case value-2:
        block-2;
        break;
case value-3:
        block-3;
        break;
case value-4:
        block-4;
        break;
default:
        default-block;
        break;
}
```

The value of this **expression** is either generated during program execution or read in as user input. The case whose value is the same as that of the **expression** is selected and executed. The optional **default** label is used to specify the code segment to be executed when the value of the expression does not match with any of the case values.

The break statement is used at the end of every case. If it were not so, the execution would continue on into the code segment of the next case

UNIT-III Statement

without even checking the case value. **For example**, supposing a switch statement has five cases and the value of the third case matches the value of **expression**. If no break statement were present at the end of the third case, all the cases after case 3 would also get executed along with case 3. If break is present only the required case is selected and executed; after which the control gets transferred to the next statement immediately after the switch statement. There is no break after default because after the default case the control will either way get transferred to the next statement immediately after switch.

Short Example

int i = 1;

switch(i)

   {

   case 1:

      printf("A");   // No break

   case 2:

      printf("B");   // No break

   case 3:

      printf("C");

   break;

   }

Output: A B C

The output was supposed to be only **A** because only the first case matches, but as there is no break statement after the block, the next blocks are executed, until the cursor encounters a break.

Rules for using switch statements:

- Case Label must be unique.
- Case Labels must end with Colon (:)
- Case labels must have constants / constant expression
- Case label must be of integral Type (Integer ,Character)
- Switch case should have at most one default label
- Default label is Optional; it is up to the user.
- Default can be placed anywhere in the switch
- Break Statement takes control out of the switch
- Two or more cases may share one break statement
- Nesting (switch within switch) is allowed.
- Relational Operators (Expression) are not allowed in Switch Statement.
- Empty Switch case is allowed.

Prog# 3.22: Write a Menu driven Program for addition, substraction, multiplication & division.

```
/*Menu Driven Program in C*/
#include <stdio.h>
#include <conio.h>
void main()
    {
    int a,b,c, option ;
    clrscr();
    printf("Enter the value of A ::");
    scanf("%d", &a);
    printf("Enter the value of B ::");
    scanf("%d", &b);
    printf ("-------------****-------------");
    printf ("\n 1: Addition");
    printf ("\n 2: Multiplication");
    printf ("\n 3: Subtraction");
```

UNIT-III
Statement

```c
        printf ("\n 4: Division");
        printf ("\n-------------****-------------\n");
        printf("Enter Your Option ::");
        scanf("%d", &option);
        switch(option)
                {
                case 1:
                        {
                        c = a + b;
                        printf(" %d + %d = %d", a,b,c);
                        break;
                        }
                case 2:
                        {
                        c = a * b;
                        printf(" %d * %d = %d", a,b,c);
                        break;
                        }
                case 3:
                        {
                        c = a - b;
                        printf(" %d - %d = %d", a,b,c);
                        break;
                        }
                case 4:
                        {
                        c = a / b;
                        printf(" %d / %d = %d", a,b,c);
                        break;
                        }
                default:
                        printf("Sorry !! You have chosen a wrong option!!");
                }
        getch();
        }
```

OUTPUT

```
Enter the value of  A:: 24
Enter the value of  B:: 42

-------------****-------------
 1: Addition
 2: Multiplication
 3: Subtraction
4: Division
-------------****-------------
Enter your option = 1

Sum is =66
```

```
Enter the value of  A:: 6
Enter the value of  B:: 5

-------------****-------------
 1: Addition
 2: Multiplication
 3: Subtraction
4: Division
-------------****-------------
Enter your option = 2

Multiplication of  two number  is =30
```

```
Enter the value of  A:: 6
Enter the value of  B:: 5

-------------****-------------
 1: Addition
 2: Multiplication
```

3: Subtraction

4: Division

-------------****-------------

Enter your option = 3

Difference of two number is =1

Enter the value of A:: 6
Enter the value of B:: 2

-------------****-------------

1: Addition

2: Multiplication

3: Subtraction

4: Division

-------------****-------------

Enter your option = 4

Difference of two number is =3

Enter the value of A:: 6
Enter the value of B:: 5

-------------****-------------

1: Addition

2: Multiplication

3: Subtraction

4: Division

-------------****-------------

Enter your option = 8

Sorry!! You have chosen a wrong option!!

Prog# 3.23: Write a program to check whether character is vowel or consonant.

```
/*Program to check whether character is vowel or consonant*/
#include <stdio.h>
#include <conio.h>
void main()
    {
    char Ch;
    clrscr();
    printf("Enter the Character ::");
    scanf("%c", &Ch);
    switch (ch)
              {
              case 'a':
              case 'A':
              case 'e':
              case 'E':
              case 'i':
              case 'I':
              case 'o':
              case 'O':
              case 'u':
              case 'U':
                      {
                      printf("Character is a vowel.\n");
                      break;
                      }
              default:
                      printf("Character is consonant.\n");
              }    //End of switch
    getch();
    }
```

OUTPUT

```
Enter the Character:: c
Character is consonant.
```

3.6 Scope Rule

Scope rule is one of the very important parts of any programming language; basically it deals with variable and uses of that variable. By the help of scope rule, we can define the area of variable means either that variable is used inside the block or outside the block. Basically there are two types of scope in C:

- ✓ Local Scope or Local Variable
- ✓ Global Scope or Global Variable

Local Variable

Local Variables are the variables declared inside a block or a main function. Since the variable declared and used locally, so that it is called as local variables. Local variables can only be used inside a block or a function where the variables are declared. Outside that function or block it becomes unknown and it will be destroyed after exiting that function or block.

So if you want to use a variable only for limited time or only for some specific purpose or only for some place or in some function or in some block, then simply use the local variable.

```
void main()
    {
    int I;   // Local Variable
    }
```

Global Variable

Global variables are the variables which are defined outside of a function, usually on top of the program i.e. above the main () function. Global variable known throughout the program. A global variable holds their values throughout the program. So the Global variables are accessible throughout the program from outside the functions or blocks to inside the functions or blocks. In short, you can access global variable from anywhere in the program.

Important - In case if the name of the global variable and local variable will be same, then the priority will first goes to the local variable. It means first local variable will be used.

int a,b;   // Global Variable

void main()

    {

    int I;   // Local Variable

    }

3.7 Storage Class

While declaring variable, our main concern is type declaration of that variable. Generally, storage classes define where our variable would be stored. A storage class defines the scope (visibility) and life-time of variables and/or functions within a C Program. All variables defined in a C program get some physical location in memory where variable's value would be stored. Memory and CPU registers are types of memory locations where a variable's value can be stored. The storage class of a variable in C determines the life time of the variable if this is 'global' or 'local'. Along with the life time of a variable, storage class also determines variable's storage location (memory or registers), the scope (visibility level) of the variable, and the initial value of the variable.

UNIT-III Statement

Types of Storage Classes

There are four storage classes in C they are as follows:

1. Automatic Storage Class
2. Register Storage Class
3. Static Storage Class
4. External Storage Class

All storage class consists of 4 common things, which are:

Storage Classes	Storage Place	Default Value	Scope	Life-time
auto	Memory	Garbage Value	Local	Within function
extern	Memory	Zero	Global	Till the end of main program, May be declared anywhere in the program
static	Memory	Zero	Local	Till the end of main program, Retains value between multiple functions call
register	Register	Garbage Value	Local	Within function

Auto Storage Class Example

```
#include <stdio.h>
void main( )
    {
      auto int i = 10;
         {
           auto int i = 11;
             {
```

```
                auto int i = 12;
                printf ( "\n%d ", i);
                }
            printf ( "%d ", i);
            }
        printf( "%d\n", i);
    }
```

OUTPUT
======
12 11 10

Register Storage Class Example

The register variable allocates memory in register than RAM. Its size is same of register size. It has a faster access than any other variables. It is recommended to use register variable only for quick access like in loops.

register int i=0;

Static Storage Class Example

The **static** variable is initialized only once and used till the end of the program. It retains its value between multiple functions call.

```
#include <stdio.h>

void staticExample()
{
  static int i;
  {
    static int i = 10;
    printf("%d ", i);
    i++;
  }
  printf("%d\n", i);
  i++;
}
```

```
int main()
{
  staticExample ();
  staticExample ();
}
```

```
OUTPUT
=======
10 0
11 1
```

External Storage Class Example

The extern variable is visible to all the programs. It can be used throuout the program.

extern int i;

By default global variable is also come in external storage class.

———•———

UNIT - IV

ARRAY & FUNCTIONS

4.1 Array Introduction

As we have seen, so far, in some programming example, we have used individual variables to store and display information. But there are some situations, where we required dealing with groups of variables. Consider a situation, where we want to store the age of five students. In this case, if the programmer uses five individual variables to store the age of student's, then its fine, but now after some time, size of student's is growing and now there are 100 students in a class. Now let's assume we have to store 100 student's age. Are we going to use 100 variables? So now if the programmer uses 100 variables, then it is not an efficient way to store the information. This type of problem can be handled in C programming using arrays. Where we have deal with group of values.

An array is a collection of similar type of data which are stored in sequential memory location under a common name or a variable name. In other words, we can say, an array is a group of values referred to by the same variable name. Arrays are useful because instead of having to separately store related information in different variables (named memory locations), you can store them—as a collection—in just one variable. The individual values in an array are called element.

Instead of declaring individual variables, such as var1, var 2, ..., var 99, you just declare one array variable **Age** of integer type and use Age[0], Age[1], and ..., Age[99] to represent individual variables. Here, 0, 1, 2, ...99 are **index** associated with **var** variable and they are being used to represent individual elements available in the array. In C, square brackets appear around the index right after the name, with the first element referred to by the number.

All arrays consist of contiguous memory locations. The lowest address corresponds to the first element and the highest address to the last element. Arrays are of three types:

- ✓ One-dimensional arrays
- ✓ Two-dimensional arrays

One- Dimensional Array

One dimensional array is an array having only one subscript variable and it is also called as a linear array. In C program like other variable, the array must be declared before one uses it. While declaring an array, we must provide following information to the compiler:

- ✓ Type of the array (i.e., integer, character, floating type etc.)
- ✓ Name of the array
- ✓ Number of subscript/dimension of the array
- ✓ Total number of the element (Maximum value of each subscript)

The syntax of 1-D array is:

Data_type array_name [size];

Where data type specifies the type of the element that will be contained in the array, such as int, float, or char and the size indicates the maximum number of elements that can be stored inside the array. Array_name is the name of the array.

Following are the some valid one dimensional array declaration is:

int Age [100];

float Per [200];

char Alpha [10];

Some invalid one dimensional array declaration is:
int Age [0];

int Per [65.2];

float Age [100];

char Name [#];

Initializations of 1-D Array

The following declares and initialization an array, which stored the age of five students. Here, we have set the value corresponding to each array element. C arrays are always indexed from 0. So the first integer in 'Age' array is Age[0] and the last is Age[4].

UNIT-IV   Array & Functions

int Age [5];

Age [0] = 18;   // set first element
Age [1] = 17;   // set second element
Age [2] = 18;   // set third element
Age [3] = 21;   // set fourth element
Age [4] = 25;   // set fifth element

This array contains 5 elements. Any one of these elements may be referred to by giving the name of the array followed by the position number of the particular element in square brackets ([]). The first element in every array is the zeroth element. Thus, the first element of array 'Age' is referred to as numbers[0], the second element of array 'Age' referred to as numbers[1], the third element of array 'Age' is referred to as numbers[2], the fourth element of array 'Age' is referred to as numbers[3], the fifth element of array 'Age' is referred to as numbers[5], and, in general, the n-th element of array 'numbers' is referred to as numbers[n - 1].

If array size is 10, then subscript is [9].

Other Examples are:

float Per [5] = { 45.54 , 78.24 , 59.64 , 84.21 , 91.45} ;
char Sex [3] = { 'M' , 'F' , ' O' } ;
char Name [5] ={ 'S' , 'O' , 'N' , 'I' , 'A'} ;

Result of above initializations is:

Per [0] = 45.54 ;
Per [1] = 78.24 ;

Per [2] = 59.64 ;
Per [3] = 84.21 ;
Per [4] = 91.25 ;

Sex [0] = 'M' ;
Sex [1] = 'F' ;
Sex [2] = 'O' ;

Name [0] = 'S' ;
Name [0] = 'O' ;
Name [0] = 'N' ;
Name [0] = 'I' ;
Name [0] = 'A' ;

Consider one more situation, where age of five students is declared but we have initialized only three elements. Now in this case, compiler will automatically set the remaining values to zero. For example,

int Age [5] = { 41 , 27 , 34};

Age [0] = 41 ;

Age [1] = 27 ;

Age [2] = 34 ;

Age [3] = 0 ;

Age [4] = 0 ;

Storing and Total Size of Array

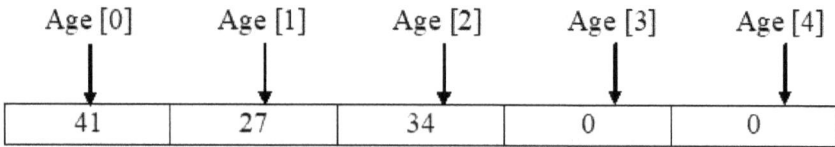

Figure: 4.1

In above, Age [5] having integer data type. We know very well that size of an integer variable is 2 bytes. So size of an above array is:

| UNIT-IV | Array & Functions |

Total Size = Data_Type Size * Total Element

Total Size = 2 * 5 = 10

If memory address of first element is 100, then next address will be 102, 104, 106 and 110.

For floating data type, total size of five elements is:

Total Size = 4 * 5 = 20

If memory address of first element is 100, then next address will be 104, 108, 112 and 116.

For character data type, total size of five elements is:

Total Size = 1 * 5 = 5

If memory address of first element is 100, then next address will be 101, 102, 103 and 104.

Prog # 4.1 Write a program to calculate the sum of 5 numbers.

```
                /*Program to calculate sum of 5 numbers*/
#include <stdio.h>
#include <conio.h>
void main()
    {
    int a[5], Sum =0 , I ;
    clrscr();
    printf(" Enter Five Elements :\n ");
    for(I=0;I<=4;I++)
        {
          scanf("%d", &a[i]);
        }
    for(I=0;I<=4;I++)
        {
        Sum= Sum + a [I];
        }
```

```
printf("\n Sum of five number is = %d", Sum);
getch();
}
```

OUTPUT

```
Enter Five Elements:
7
5
6
8
6
Sum of five elements is: 32
```

On the above program, we have used for loop. It is very important that, while using array, we always prefer to use loop. For storing the value of an array and for retrieving the value from the array, we always use loop because we know that the array index will start from the 0 and end with n-1.

On above, for loop statement:

```
for (i =0;i<=4;i++)
    {
    scanf("%d", &a [i]) ;
    }
```

Where,
    i=0 , a [0] =7
    i=1 , a [1] =5
    i=2 , a [2] =6
    i=3 , a [3] =8
    i=4 , a [4] =6

We have used one more loop in Result () function, because this loop used to get values from the memory location and perform sum operation.

Where,

| UNIT-IV | Array & Functions |

i=0 , Sum = Sum + a[i] , Sum= 0 + a[0] , Sum = 0 + 7 ;
Sum = 7
    i=1 , Sum = Sum + a[i] , Sum= 7 + a[1] , Sum = 7 + 5 ;
Sum = 12
    i=2 , Sum = Sum + a[i] , Sum= 12 + a[2] , Sum = 12 + 6 ;
Sum = 18
    i=3 , Sum = Sum + a[i] , Sum= 18 + a[3] , Sum = 18 + 8 ;
Sum = 26
    i=4 , Sum = Sum + a[i] , Sum= 26 + a[4] , Sum = 26 + 6 ;
Sum = 32

Prog # 4.2 **Write a program to find out the greatest number from array elements.**

```
                /*Program to calculate sum of 5 numbers*/
#include <stdio.h>
#include <conio.h>
void main()
    {
    int a[100], No , I ;
    clrscr();
    printf("Enter Size of an Array ::");
    scanf("%d",&No);
    for(I=0;I<=No-1;I++)
        {
        printf("Enter [%d] Element::", I+1);
        scanf("%d", &a[I]);
        }
    for(I=0;i<=No-1;++I)
        {
        if(a[0]<a[i])
            {
                a[0]=a[i];
            }
```

        }
    printf("\nLargest element is :: %d",a[0]);
    getch();
}

OUTPUT

```
Enter Size of an array: 7

Enter [ 1 ] Element :: 21
Enter [ 2 ] Element :: 27
Enter [ 3 ] Element :: 34
Enter [ 4 ] Element :: 52
Enter [ 5 ] Element :: 67
Enter [ 6 ] Element :: 56
Enter [ 7 ] Element :: 59

Largest Element is :: 67
```

On the above program, below statement is the most important part:

```
for(i=0;i<n;++i)
    {
    if(a[0]<a[i])
        a[0]=a[i];
    }
```

Initially we have assumed that, the first element is the greatest and after that, on each iteration, we compare first element with next element. If the next element is greater than previous one, then that value assign into a[0]. This process is running till the end of loop and at last greatest value among array element is stored into a [0].

Prog # 4.3 Write a program to search an element from the array list.

/*Program to Search an Element from Array*/
#include <stdio.h>
#include <conio.h>
void main()
    {

```c
int a[100], No , I, Search, Find = 1;
clrscr();
printf ("Enter Size of an Array ::");
scanf("%d", &No);
for(I=0;I<=No-1;I++)
   {
      printf("Enter [%d] Element::", I+1);
      scanf("%d", &a[I]);
   }
printf("\n Enter the search element ::");
scanf("%d", &Search);
for(I=0;i<=No-1;++I)
   {
     if(a[I]==Search)
        {
          Find=0;
            break;
        }
   }
  if(Find= =0)
   {
      printf("Number is found !!!!");
   }
  else
     {
    printf("Number is not found !!");
   }
  getch();
}
```

OUTPUT

```
Enter Size of an array: 8

Enter [ 1 ] Element :: 21
Enter [ 2 ] Element :: 27
Enter [ 3 ] Element :: 34
```

```
Enter [ 4 ] Element :: 52
Enter [ 5 ] Element :: 67
Enter [ 6 ] Element :: 56
Enter [ 7 ] Element :: 59
Enter [ 8 ] Element :: 121

Enter the search number: 67
Number is found !!!!
```

On the above program, we have not written output statement inside loop. Inside the loop, either condition is true or false. Suppose the array size is 100, and we have entered 100 numbers and some of the number is repeated in the list. Now if the search element is matched in array list, and that element is on 95th position, then 94 times false statement is executed and after that correct statement which is number is found executed. But obviously, it is not a desired output of the program. We want to output in a single statement, either found or not found. For this purpose, we have initialized a variable 'Find' to 1 because, if the search element is found, then value of 'Find' variable is changed and set to 0.

Two-Dimensional Array

Two-dimensional array is a simple data structure for organizing tabular data. Two-dimensional array are those type of array, which has finite number of rows and finite number of columns. A two dimensional array (will be written 2-D hereafter) can be imagined as a matrix or table of rows and columns or as an array of one dimensional array.

The declaration form of 2-dimensional array is:

Data_type Array_name [row size][column size];

The type may be any valid type supported by C++. The rule for giving the array name is same as the ordinary variable. The row size and column size should be an individual constant.

For Example:

int a [2] [3];   // Two rows and three columns
int a [3] [3];   //Three rows and three columns

| UNIT-IV | Array & Functions |

First subscript represents rows & second subscript represents columns. Like 1-D array, both the subscript from 2-D array will be start at index 0.

Initialization of 2D Array

There are many ways to initialize two Dimensional arrays –

```
int a [2][4] = {
   {10, 11, 12, 13},
   {14, 15, 16, 17}
};
```

OR

int a [2][4] = { 10, 11, 12, 13, 14, 15, 16, 17};

Above initialization stored in a tabular format, like:

	Column 1	Column 2	Column 3	Column 4
Row 1	a [0] [0]	a [0] [1]	a [0] [2]	a [0] [3]
Row 2	a [1] [0]	a [1] [1]	a [1] [2]	a [1] [3]

Above values stored in following way:

	Column 1	Column 2	Column 3	Column 4
Row 1	10	11	12	13
Row 2	14	15	16	17

In the above example, initializations of the 2-D array stored in memory sequentially. We can create a memory block in the multiplication of rows and column. For example, If a [3] [4] is array declaration, then memory consist of 12 blocks.

However the actual representation of above array in memory would be something like-

A[0][0]	A[0][1]	A[0][2]	A[0][3]	A[1][0]	A[1][1]	A[1][2]	A[1][3]
10	11	12	13	14	15	16	17

Row1   Row2

You must remember that when we give values during one dimensional array declaration, we don't need to mention dimension. But that's not the case with 2-D array; you must specify the second dimension even if you are giving values during the declaration. Let's understand this with the help of few examples –

/* Valid declaration*/
int a [2][2] = {1, 2, 3 ,4 }

/* Valid declaration*/
int a[][2] = {1, 2, 3 ,4 }

/* Invalid declaration – you must specify second dimension*/
int a[][] = {1, 2, 3 ,4 }
/* Invalid because of the same reason mentioned above*/
int a[2][] = {1, 2, 3 ,4 }

Prog # 4.4 Write a program for addition of two matrix using two dimensional array.

/*Program for addition of two matrix*/

```
#include <stdio.h>
#include <conio.h>
void main()
    {
    int a[3][3] , b[3][3] , c[3][3], i ,j ;
    clrscr();
    printf("Enter first matrix values :\n");
    for (i=0;i<=1;i++)
```

```
        {
            for (j=0;j<=1;j++)
                {
                    printf("Element of [ %d ] ] [ %d ] =", i , j);
                    scanf("%d",&a[i][j]);
                } // End of Inner for loop
        }// End of outer loop

    printf("\nEnter Second matrix values :\n");
    for (i=0;i<=1;i++)
        {
            for (j=0;j<=1;j++)
                {
                    printf("Element of [ %d ] ] [ %d ] =", i , j);
                    scanf("%d",&b[i][j]);
                } // End of Inner for loop
        }// End of outer loop
    printf("\n Sum of two matrix is: \n\n");
    for(i=0;i<=1;i++)
        {
            for(j=0;j<=1;j++)
                {
                    c [i] [j] = a[i] [j] + b [i] [j];
                    printf("%d\t",c [i] [j]);
                }
                printf("\n");
        }
    getch();
```

}

OUTPUT

```
Enter first matrix values:
        Element of [ 0 ][ 0 ] = 3
        Element of [ 0 ][ 1 ] = 5
        Element of [ 1 ][ 0 ] = 1
        Element of [ 1 ][ 1 ] = 7

Enter Second matrix values:
        Element of [ 0 ][ 0 ] = 5
        Element of [ 0 ][ 1 ] = 3
        Element of [ 1 ][ 0 ] = 8
        Element of [ 1 ][ 1 ] = 2
Sum of two matrix is :
        8  8
        9  9
```

In 2-D arrays, we have required two for loop for storing the information and access the values. Inner loop running till condition is true, when inner loop condition is false then again outer loop will start. As we know that in 2-D array first row represent by 0 and first column represent by 0.

I=0 , j =0   value is =3
I=0 , j =1   value is =5
I=1 , j =0   value is =1
I=1 , j= 1   value is =7

On the same way, value of second matrix is stored. When sum is required, on the above same way, value is accessed from the matrix 'a' & 'b'.

Prog # 4.5 **Write a program to find the transpose of a given matrix.**

/* Transpose of a given matrix */

#include <stdio.h>

#include <conio.h>

void main()

```c
{
    int a[3][3], i ,j , t [3] [3] , m ,n;
    clrscr();
    printf("Enter the number of rows and column :\n");
    scanf("%d,%d", m , n);
    printf("Enter first matrix values :\n");
    for (i=0;i<m;i++)
    {
        for (j=0;j<n;j++)
        {
            printf("Element of [ %d ] ] [ %d ] =", i , j);
            scanf("%d",&a[i][j]);
        }   // End of Inner for loop
    }// End of outer loop
    for (i=0;i<m;i++)
    {
        for (j=0;j<n;j++)
        {
            t [j] [i] = a [i] [j];
        }   // End of Inner for loop
    }// End of outer loop

    printf("\n Transpose of a given matrix A IS :\n");
    for (i=0;i<n;i++)
    {
        for (j=0;j<m;j++)
        {
            printf("%d \t", t[i][j]);
```

        } // **End of Inner for loop**

    printf("\n");

    }// **End of outer loop**

  getch();

}

OUTPUT

```
Enter the number of row and column: 3,3
Enter first matrix values:
            Element of [ 0 ][ 0 ] = 3
            Element of [ 0 ][ 1 ] = 5
            Element of [ 0 ][ 2 ] = 1
            Element of [ 1 ][ 0 ] = 4
            Element of [ 1 ][ 1 ] = 9
            Element of [ 1 ][ 2 ] = 7
            Element of [ 2 ][ 0 ] = 3
            Element of [ 2 ][ 1 ] = 1
            Element of [ 2 ][ 2 ] = 1

Transpose of a Given matrix A IS:
            3   4   3
            5   9   1
            1   7   1
```

4.2 Functions Introduction

A functions is a group of statements which works together to perform specific task. When we want to divide large complex program into small parts then function is always useful. All C programs must contain the function main ( ). The execution of the program starts from the function main ( ). A C program can contain any number of functions according to the needs. Depending on whether a function is predefined or created by programmer; there are two types of function:

   1. Library Function / Built-In functions

2. User-defined Function

1. Library Functions :
Library functions are the built-in function in C programming language. Programmer can use directly library function by writing appropriate header file in which function working is defined; they don't need to write it themselves. In c programming language, printf() & scanf() are input/output functions. In previous chapter we have already explain header files in detail. In C programming language, one library function must used by programmer which is main() function.

Example: Suppose we want to find out the square root of any given number so for this purpose we must use directly SQRT () function. Some of the library functions are:

A. **Standard Input / Output**

Stream	Description
printf()	standard input stream
scanf()	standard output stream

B. **Math Library Function**

Function	Description
sin(x)	Sine of an angle x (measured in radians)
cos(x)	Cosine of an angle x (measured in radians)
tan(x)	Tangent of an angle x (measured in radians)
asin(x)	Sin-1 (x) where x (measured in radians)
acos(x)	Cos-1 (x) where x (measured in radians)
exp(x)	Exponential function of x (ex)
log(x)	logarithm of x

log 10(x)	Logarithm of number x to the base 10
sqrt(x)	Square root of x, Where value of x is given by user
pow(x, y)	x raised to the power y
abs(x)	Absolute value of integer number x
fabs(x)	Absolute value of real number x

C. Character Function

Function	Description
isalpha(n)	It returns True if n is an uppercase letter and False if c is lowercase.
isdigit(n)	It returns True if n is a digit (0 through 9) otherwise False.
isalnum(n)	It returns True if n is a digit from 0 through 9 or an alphabetic character (either uppercase or lowercase) otherwise False.
islower(n)	It returns True if n is a lowercase letter otherwise False.
isupper(n)	It returns True if n is an uppercase letter otherwise False.
toupper(n)	It converts n to uppercase letter.
tolower()	It converts n to lowercase letter.

D. String Function

Function	Description
strlen()	Calculates the length of string
strcpy()	Copies a string to another string
strcat()	Concatenates(joins) two strings
strcmp()	Compares two string
strlwr()	Converts string to lowercase

strupr()	Converts string to uppercase
Strspn(str1,str2)	Returns the number of initial consecutive characters of str1 that are not in str2
Strcpn(str1,str2)	Returns the number of initial consecutive characters of str1 that are in str2

2. User-defined Functions:

A user-defined function group of code to perform a specific task and that group of code is given a name. C allows programmer to define their own function name. When that function is invoked from any part of program, it all executes the codes defined in the body of function. Programmer can give any name of function but it is always recommended that function name must be reflecting with working of function.

Syntax:

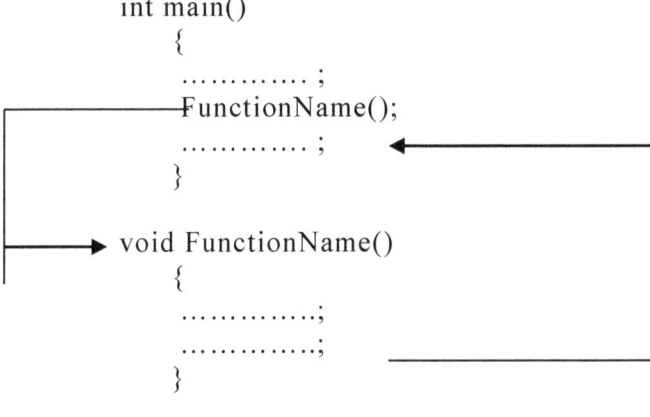

4.3 Why Functions?

Function can be used to achieve following objectives:

- ✓ The length of a source program can be reduced by using functions at appropriate places. This factor is very important when we want to use memory in effective way.

- ✓ It is easy to locate and isolate a faulty function for further investigations.

- ✓ A function may be used by many other programs. This means that a C programmer can build on what others have already done, instead of starting all over again from scratch.

- ✓ It facilitates top-down modular programming. In this programming style, the high level logic of the overall problem is solved first while the details of each lower-level function are addressed later.

Function Example

Prog#4.6: C Program to add two numbers by using function.

```c
/*This is program of sum of two number by using function*/

#include<stdio.h>
#include<conio.h>

int add(int ,int );                        // Function Prototype (Declaration)

int main()
 {
  int a,b,sum;
  clrscr();
  printf("Enter first number ::");
  scanf("%d",&a);
  printf ("Enter second number::");        → Here a & b are actual argument
  scanf("%d",&b);
  sum=add(a,b);                            //Function Call
  printf("The Sum of  %d + % d = %d ", a,b,sum);
  getch();
  return(0);                               → Here a & b are formal argument
 }

int add(int a,int b)                       // Function Definition
 {
  int total;
  total=a+b;
  return (total);                          // Return Statement
 }
```

OUTPUT

```
Enter first number ::8
Enter second number:: 9
The Sum of 8+9 = 17
```

There are 5 important parts of function:

- ✓ Function prototyping
- ✓ Function Declaration/Calling
- ✓ Function Definition
- ✓ Actual argument & formal argument
- ✓ Return Statement

Function Prototyping

In C++, function prototype is a declaration of function without function body to give information about user-defined function to compiler. If a user-defined function is defined after `main ()` function, compiler will show error. It is because compiler is unaware of user-defined function, types of argument passed to function and return type. Function prototype must match while defining body of function. Function prototype in above example:

int add(int , int);

You can see that, there is no body of function in prototype. Also there are only return type of arguments. You can also declare function prototype as below but it's not necessary to write arguments.

   int add(int a, int b);

<u>**Note**: It is not necessary to define prototype if user-defined function exists before `main ()` function.</u>

UNIT-IV   Array & Functions

Function Calling/Declaration

While creating a C function, you must give a definition of what the function has to perform task. To use a function, you will have to call that function to perform the defined work.

When a program calls a function, the program control is transferred to the called function. A called function performs a defined work and when its return statement is executed or when its function-ending closing brace is reached, it returns the program control back to the main program.

To call a function, you simply need to pass the required parameters along with the function name, and if the function has returns a value, then you can store the returned value. In the above program, sum=add (a,b); inside main() function calls the user-defined function. In the above program, user-defined function returns an integer which is stored in variable *sum*.

Function Definition
Function definition is places where we have define actual working of function. At the time of definition of a function actual logic is implemented with-in the function.

The general form of a function definition in C++ is as follows:

function-type function-name (parameter-list)
       {
        local-definitions;
        function-implementation;
       }

- If the function returns a value then the type of that value must be specified in *function-type*. This could be int, float or char. If the function does not return a value then the *function-type* must be void.

- The *function-name* follows the same rules of composition as identifiers.
- The *parameter-list* lists the formal parameters of the function together with their types.
- The *local-definitions* are definitions of variables that are used in the *function-implementation*. These variables have no meaning outside the function.
- The *function-implementation* consists of C++ executable statements that implement the effect of the function.

On above example function definition is:

```
int add(int a,int b)
  {
  int total;
  total=a+b;              //Logic for adding two numbers
  return (total);
  }
```

Actual Arguments & Formal Arguments

In function, actual argument & formal argument are the most important part. Actual arguments are those arguments which are declared inside main function. Formal arguments are those arguments which are declared while working of function is defined. Return types & number of arguments must be same in actual & formal arguments. Value of actual argument is copy into formal argument & there are two way of passing value from actual argument into formal argument:

- **Call by value:** This method copies the actual value of an argument into the formal argument of the function.

- **Call by references:** This method copies the address of an argument into the formal parameter. Inside the function, the address is used to access the actual argument used in the call.

While passing arguments we must remember below points:

- The numbers of actual arguments and formals argument should be same.
- The type of first actual argument should match with the type of first formal argument. Similarly, type of second actual argument should match with the type of second formal argument and so on.
- You may call function without passing any argument. The number(s) of argument passed to a function depends on how programmer wants to solve the problem.
- In above program, both arguments are of int type. But it's not necessary to have both arguments of same type.

Return Statement

A function can return single value to the calling program using return statement. In the above program, the value of *total* is returned from user-defined function to the calling program using statement below:

return (total);

Function return type and the variable which we have used in return statement must be same. On above program, function return type is int & total is also a type of int. If no value is returned to the calling function then, void should be used.

```
int main()
{
    .................. ;
    Sum=add(a,b);
    .................. ;
    .................. ;
}

int add(int a,int b)                          // Function Definition
{
    int total;
    total=a+b;
    return (total);                           // Return Statement
}
```

Calling a function by using call by value

In call by value, same value of actual argument is copied into formal argument means Xerox copy of actual argument is created pass into the formal argument. So if the data passed (that is stored in the function variable) is modified inside the function, the value is only changed in the variable used inside the function.

Prog#4.7: C Program to subtract two numbers by using call by value.

/*This is program of sum of two number by using function*/

```c
#include<stdio.h>
#include<conio.h>

int Sub(int ,int );            // Function Prototype (Declaration)

int main()
 {
  int a,b,Diff;
  clrscr();
  printf("Enter first number ::");
  scanf("%d",&a);
  printf ("Enter second number::");
  scanf("%d",&b);
  Diff=Sub(a,b);                //Function Call
  printf("The Subtraction of %d - % d = %d ", a,b,Diff);
  getch();
  return(0);
 }


int Sub(int X,int Y)            // Function Definition
 {
  int Difference;
  Difference =X - Y;
  return (Difference);          // Return Statement
 }
```

OUTPUT

Enter first number ::11
Enter second number:: 9
The Subtraction of 11-9 = 2

Explanation:

In above program, a & b are the actual argument. X & Y are the formal arguments. Now in call by value exact copy of a & b means value of 11 &9 is copied to formal argument x & y. So x & y is just used the value of a & b.

In call by value, one very important point is any update made inside function definition will not affect the **original value of variable in calling function**.

Example:

```
#include<stdio.h>
#include<conio.h>

void Alter(int );
int main()
   {
   int a=10;
   clrscr();
   printf(" a=%d before function call::\n",a);
   Alter(a);
   printf(" a=%d after function call::\n",a);
   getch();
   return (0);
   }

Void Alter(int x)
    {
    printf(" X=%d before adding 10\n",x);
    x=x+10;
    printf(" X=%d after adding 10\n",x);
    }
```

| UNIT-IV | Array & Functions |

OUTPUT

```
a=10 before function call
X=10 before adding 10
X=20 after adding 10
a=10 after function call
```

Explanation:

Let's take a look at what is happening in this call-by-value source code example. In the main () we create 'a' integer that has the value of 10. We print some information at every stage, beginning by printing our variable 'a'. Then function Alter () is called and we input the variable a. This variable (a) is then copied to the function variable x. In the function we add 10 to 'x' (and also call some print statements). Then when the next statement is called in main () the value of variable 'a' is printed. We can see that the value of variable a isn't changed by the call of the function Alter ().So after execution of this program, it is Cleary visible that there is no change happened inside main function.

Prog#4.8: C Program to demonstrate multi-function in single program.

/*This is program of sum of two number by using function*/

```c
#include<stdio.h>
#include<conio.h>

int Sum(int,int,int);      // Function prototype for sum of three number
int Mul(int,int,int);      // Function prototype for multiplication of three number

int main()
{
    int a,b,c,Add,Mult;
    clrscr();
    printf("Enter the value of A ::");
    scanf("%d",&a);
    printf ("Enter the value of B::");
    scanf("%d",&b);
    printf("Enter the value of C::");
    scanf("%d",&c);
    Add=Sum(a,b,c);                         //Function Call
    printf("\nThe Sum of Three Number Is= %d ",Add);
    Mult=Mul(a,b,c);                        //Function Call
    printf("\n\nThe Multiplication of Three Number Is= %d ", Mult);

    getch();
    return(0);
}

/*Function definition of Sum*/

int Sum(int X,int Y, int Z)
{
    int total;
    total =X + Y + Z;
    return (total);                         // Return Statement
}
/*Function definition of multiplication*/

int Mul(int X,int Y, int Z)
```

OUTPUT

Enter the value of A:: 5
Enter the value of B:: 4
Enter the value of C:: 3

The Sum of Three Number Is ::12

The Multiplication of Three Number Is ::60

Explanation:

In the above program, firstly function definition of sum is executed and then it jumps back to the main function. After printing the result of the sum then the function of multiplication is executed and then it jumps back to the main function. Multi-functional is always useful when our program contains more than 2 operations like in above program because if any parts contain error then programmer tries to correct only that part. Assume that we want to create a program for prime numbers, the factorial of a number & Fibonacci series so instead of writing three programs we can create three functions for each operation in a single program. It saves time & also it will provide an efficient way of memory utilization.

Prog#4.9: Write a program to find out square & cube of given number using function.

```
/*This is program for square & cube using function*/

#include<stdio.h>
#include<conio.h>
int Square(int);            //Function prototype for Square
int Cube(int);              //Function prototype for cube
int S;                      //Global variable
int main()
 {
   int n;
   int Sq,Cu;
   clrscr();
   printf("Enter the value of N ::");
   scanf("%d",&n);
   Sq= Square (n);
   printf(Square of %d is = %d, n , Sq);
   Cu= Cube (n);
   printf(Cube of %d is = %d, n , Sq);
   getch();
   return(0);
 }
int Square(int n)           //Function definition of Square
 {
   S=n*n;
   return(S);
 }
int Cube(int x)             //Function definition of Cube
 {
   int C;
   C=x*S;
   return(C);
 }
```

OUTPUT

```
Enter the value of N ::3
Square of 3 Is =9

Cube of 3 Is=27
```

On above program, we have declare S as a global variable because the result of S is used in cube function. This is important for effective use of memory.

Prog#4.10: Write a program to find out factorial of given number using function.

/*This is program for factorial of given number*/

```
#include<stdio.h>
#include<conio.h>
int Fact(int);              //Function prototype for Factorial
int main()
   {
    int n, i, F;
    clrscr();
    printf("Enter the value of N ::");
    scanf("%d",&n);
    F = Fact (n);
    getch();
    return(0);
   }
/*Function definition of factorial*/
int Fact(int n)
   {
    int F=1,i;
    for(i=1;i<=n;i++)
       {
        F=F*i;
       }
    return(F);
   }
```

OUTPUT

```
Enter the Number ::5
Factorial of 5 Is =120
```

Prog#4.11: Write a program to find out multiplication table of given number using function.

/*This is a program of multiplication table of given number using function*/

```c
#include<stdio.h>
#include<conio.h>
void Table(int);                //Function prototype for Table
int main()
   {
    int n ;
    clrscr();
    printf("Enter the value of N ::");
    scanf("%d",&n);
    Table (n);
    getch();
    return(0);
   }

void Table(int N)
   {
    int i,Result;
    for(i=1;i<=10;i++)
       {
        Result=N*i;
        Printf("%d * %d = %d",N,i, Result);
       }
   }
```

OUTPUT

```
Enter the Value of N ::4
4 * 1=4
4 * 2=8
4 * 3=12
4 * 4=16
4 * 5=20
4 * 6=24
4 * 7=28
4 * 8=32
4 * 9=36
4 * 10=40
```

4.4 Recursion

When a function called itself is known as recursive function. And, this technique is known as recursion. A useful way to think of recursive functions is to imagine them as a process being performed where one of the instructions is to "repeat the process". This makes it sound very similar to a loop because it repeats the same code again & again, and in some ways it *is* similar to looping. On the other hand, recursion makes it easier to express ideas in which the result of the recursive call is necessary to complete the task. Of course, it must be possible for the "process" to sometimes be completed without the recursive call. One simple example is the idea of building a wall that is twelve feet high; if I want to build a twelve foot high wall, and then I will first build an 11 foot high wall, and then add an extra foot of bricks. Conceptually, this is like saying the "build wall" function takes a height and if that height is greater than one, first calls itself to build a lower wall, and then adds one a foot of bricks.

Practical Example of C Recursion

What's the practical use of recursion? In this section, I will provide some practical examples where recursion can makes things really easy.

Suppose you have numbers from 0 to 9 and you need to calculate the sum of these numbers in the following way:

UNIT-IV   Array & Functions

0 + 1 = 1

1 + 2 = 3

3 + 3 = 6

6 + 4 = 10

10 + 5 = 15

15 + 6 = 21

21 + 7 = 28

28 + 8 = 36

36 + 9 = 45

So, you can see that we start with 0 and 1, sum them up and add the result into next number i.e. 2 then again we add this result to 3 and continue like this.

Now, I will show you how recursion can be used to define logic for this requirement in a C code:

```c
#include <stdio.h>
#include<conio.h>

int count = 1;
void Func(int sum)
{
   sum  = sum + count;
   count ++;

   if(count <= 9)
     {
     Func(sum);
     }
   else
     {
     printf("Sum is= %d\n",sum);
     }
}
```

If you try to understand what the above code does, you will observe:

- ✓ When Func() was called through main(), 'sum' was zero.
- ✓ For every call to Func(), the value of 'sum' is incremented with 'count' (which is 1 initially), which itself gets incremented with every call.
- ✓ The condition of termination of this recursion is when value of 'count' exceeds 9. This is exactly what we expect.
- ✓ When 'count' exceeds 9, at this very moment, the value of 'sum' is the final figure that we want and hence the solution.

NOTE:

- ✓ Recursion makes program better and cleaner. All algorithms can be defined recursively which makes it easier to visualize and prove.
- ✓ If the speed of the program is important then, you should avoid using recursion. Recursions use more memory and are generally slow.

Prog#4.12: Write a program to find the sum of natural number using recursion.

/*This is program for sum of natural number using recursion*/

```
#include <stdio.h>
#include<conio.h>
int Sum(int n);
int main()
   {
    int Number, Result;
    clrscr();
    printf("Enter a positive integer::");
    scanf("%d", &Number);
    Result = Sum(number);
    printf("sum= %d", Result);
   }
int Sum(int n)
   {
   if (n!=0)
      return n + Sum(n-1);         // sum() function calls itself
   else
      return (n);
   }
```

OUTPUT

Enter a positive integer::*3*
Sum=6

Explanation:

```
int main() {
... .. ...                3
result = sum(number)
... .. ...
}

int sum(int n)                         3+3 = 6
{                                      is returned
    if(n!=0)     3          2
        return n + sum(n-1);
    else
        return n;
}
                                       1+2 = 3
int sum(int n)                         is returned
{
    if(n!=0)     2          1
        return n + sum(n-1);
    else
        return;
}
                                       0+1 = 1
int sum(int n)                         is returned
{
    if(n!=0)     1          0
        return n + sum(n-1);
    else
        return n;
}

int sum(int n)
{                                      0
    if(n!=0)                           is returned
        return n + sum(n-1);
    else
        return n;
}
```

Fig. 4.1

Prog#4.13: C++ program to find the factorial of given number using recursion.

```c
/* Program to find factorial of a given number using recursion */
#include <stdio.h>
#include<conio.h>
int Factorial(int);

int main()
   {
   int Num,Result;
   clrscr();
   printf("Enter a number to find it's Factorial:: ");
   scanf("%d", &Num);
   if (Num < 0)
      {
      printf ("Factorial of negative number not possible\n");
      }
   else
      {
      Result = Factorial (Num);
      printf("The Factorial of %d Is = %d ", Num, Result);
      }
   getch();
   return 0;
}
int Factorial(int num)
   {
   if (num == 0 || num == 1)
      {
      return (1);
      }
   else
      {
      return(num * Factorial(num - 1));        // Recursive logic
      }
}
```

OUTPUT

```
Enter a number to find it's Factorial:: 5
The factorial of 5 Is=120
```

Prog#4.14: Write a program to find power of number using recursion.

```c
/* This is a Program to find Power of a Number using Recursion */
#include <stdio.h>
#include<conio.h>
long Power (int, int);

int main()
{
int Pow, Num;
clrscr();
long Result;
printf("Enter a number: ");
scanf("%d", &Num);
printf ("Enter its power: ");
scanf("%d", &Pow);
Result = Power(Num,Pow);
printf<<"Power of %d^%d Is = %d", Pow, Num, Result);
getch();
return (0);
}

//Function definition of power function
long Power (int num, int pow)
    {
    if (pow)                    //Condition true for only non-zero value
        {
            return (num * power(num, pow - 1));
        }
    return 1;
    }
```

UNIT-IV   Array & Functions

OUTPUT

```
Enter a number: 3
Enter its power:2
Power of 3^2 Is=9
```

Explanation:

When you close look at the function definition of power, if value of power is zero then result is 1 but if value of power is non zero then:

On 1st Iteration:

return (num * power(num, pow - 1));   ➔ return(3*Power(3,1))

On 2nd Iteration:

return (num * power(num, pow - 1));   ➔ return(3*3*power(3,0))

When value of power become zero then it will return 1 and answer would be 9.

Fibonacci Series Program

The Fibonacci sequence is a set of numbers that starts with a one or a zero, followed by a one, and proceeds based on the rule that each number (called a Fibonacci number) is equal to the sum of the preceding two numbers. The simplest is the series 1, 1, 2, 3, 5, 8,13,21,34 etc.

When we implement the logic of Fibonacci series, then it looks simple because we add two previous number and then swap with new number, but in this implementation, we must use a number which is used to stop Fibonacci series. Suppose the value of n is 10 then: 0 1 1 2 3 5 8 13 21 34.

Below we are giving two logics of above method by using recursion.

Prog#4.15: Write a program for Fibonacci series using recursion. **(Logic-I)**

/*Fibonacci series using recursion*/

```
#include<stdio.h>
#include<conio.h>

void PrintFibonacci(int);

int main()
 {
  clrscr();
  int n;
  int i=0,j=1;
  printf"Enter the range of the Fibonacci series: ");
  scanf("%d",&n);
  printf("Fibonacci Series: ");
  printf(" %d   %d", i , j);
  PrintFibonacci(n);
  getch();
  return (0);
 }

void PrintFibonacci(int n)
   {
    int First=0,Second=1,Sum;
    while(n>0)
       {
        Sum = First + Second;
        First = Second;
        Second = Sum;
        printf("%d",Sum);
        n--;
       }
   }
```

| UNIT-IV | Array & Functions |

OUTPUT

```
Enter the range of the Fibonacci series: 10
Fibonacci Series: 0 1 1 2 3 5 8 13 21 34 55 89
```

Prog#4.16: Write a program for Fibonacci series using recursion. **(Logic-II)**

/*Fibonacci series using recursion*/

```c
#include<stdio.h>
#include<conio.h>

int Fibonacci(int);

int main()
   {
   clrscr();
   int n, i = 0, j,Result;
   printf("Enter the range of the Fibonacci series: ");
   scanf("%d",&n);
   printf("Fibonacci Series: ");
   for ( j = 1 ; j <= n ; j++ )
       {
          Result= Fibonacci(i);
          printf("%d",Result;
          j++;
       }
   getch();
   return (0);
   }

int Fibonacci(int n)
   {
   if ( n == 0 )
      return 0;
   else if ( n == 1 )
      return 1;
   else
      return ( Fibonacci(n-1) + Fibonacci(n-2) );
   }
```

OUTPUT

Enter the range of the Fibonacci series: 10
Fibonacci Series: 0 1 1 2 3 5 8 13 21 34 55 89

NOTE:

In this unit, the entire program is implemented without class & object but it is always recommended that implement every program by using class & object. In this unit, our goal is to clear all the concept of function with proper implementation of logics.

4.6 Pointers Introduction

When writing a program, you declare the necessary variables that you will need in order to accomplish your work. When declaring variables, you are simply asking the computer to reserve a amount of space in its memory for a particular object you want to use. When you declare a variable, the computer reserves an amount of space for that variable, and uses the variable's name to refer to that memory space. This will allow you to store something, namely the value of that variable, in that space. Indeed, the computer refers to that space using an address. Therefore, everything you declare has an address, just like the address of your house. You can find out what address a particular variable is using.

For a C program, the memory of a computer is like a succession of memory cells, each one byte in size, and each with a unique address. These single-byte memory cells are ordered in a way that allows data representations larger than one byte to occupy memory cells that have consecutive addresses. This way, each cell can be easily located in the memory by means of its unique address. For example, the memory cell with the address 1006 always follows immediately after the cell with address 1005 and precedes the one with 1007, and is exactly one thousand cells after 0006 and exactly one thousand cells before 2006.

If you want to know the address of variable, then we must write below code:

```
#include <stdio.h>
int main()
    {
    int value;
```

```
printf ("Value Address is:: %x" ,&value);
printf( "\n\n");
return 0;
}
```

You could get: 0x0075ADF4

Output of above code is different each time on compilation. We have used **&** operator to get address of variable.

What is Pointers?

Pointer is the variables, which takes the address of another variable. Pointer variable always point to the memory location of variable. Some C tasks are performed more easily with pointers, and other C tasks, such as dynamic memory allocation, cannot be performed without them. Pointers are not particularly useful when declared and used inside of one function. They show their capabilities when different functions exchange data stored in those pointers. As you can see from the execution of the program above, the address of a variable is very difficult to read and interpret. Fortunately, we don't need to know that address and we don't need to know what it means or where the variable is located.

Pointers use two types of operator:

- ✓ Address- of Operator (&)
- ✓ Dereference operator (*)

The & operator can find address occupied by a variable. If Value is a variable then, & Value gives the address of that variable.

Just like any other variable in C, you should declare and initialize a pointer variable before using it. To declare a pointer variable, use an identifier, followed by an asterisk (*), followed by the name of the pointer, and a semi-colon. Here is the way of declaring a pointer variable:

DataType *PointerName;

The identifier should be one of those we have studied already. This means it could be an int, a char, a double, etc. The identifier should be the same type of identifier the pointer variable will point to. Therefore, if you are declaring a pointer that will point to an integer variable, the pointer identifier should be an integer.

The asterisk (*) symbol provide an instruction to compiler, that we have use pointer variable.

Be careful when declaring more than one pointer variable. If you declare a few of them on the same line, like this:

DataType* pointer1, pointer2;

Only the first variable is a pointer, the second is a regular variable. If you want to declare different variables, you use:

DataType* pointer1, *pointer2;
Or
DataType* pointer1;

DataType* pointer2;

Since the name of the pointer is same as the name of a variable, you will follow the naming rules that follow every C variable.

Prog # 4.17 Write a program to demonstrate the use of pointers.

```
#include <stdio.h>
#include<conio.h>
void main ()
    {
    int a = 20;   /* actual variable declaration */
    int *b;       /* pointer variable declaration */

    b = &a; /* store address of var in pointer variable*/

    printf("Address of A variable: %x\n", &a );

    /* address stored in pointer variable */
    printf("Address stored in B variable: %x\n", b );
```

| UNIT-IV | Array & Functions |

```
/* access the value using the pointer */
printf("Value of *b variable: %d\n", *b );
getch();
}
```

OUTPUT

Address of A variable: bggd8b3c

Address stored in B variable: bgfd8b3c

Value of *b variable: 20

Pointer Arithmetic in C

In C pointer holds address of a value, so there can be arithmetic operations on the pointer variable. Following arithmetic operations are possible on pointer in C language:

- ✓ Increment
- ✓ Decrement
- ✓ Addition
- ✓ Subtraction

Consider below table, We have declared some of the variables and also assumed some address for declared variables and we have 32 bit machine.

Data Type	Initial Address	Operation	Address after Operations	Required Bytes
int	5000	++	5002	2
int	5000	--	4998	2
char	5000	++	5001	1

Data Type	Initial Address	Operation	Address after Operations	Required Bytes
char	5000	- -	5999	1
float	5000	++	5004	4
float	5000	- -	5996	4
long	5000	++	5004	4
long	5000	- -	5996	4

Now we can see address of an variable after performing arithmetic operations.

Expression	Result
Address + Number	Address
Address − Number	Address
Address − Address	Number
Address + Address	Illegal

Above table clearly shows that we can add or subtract address and integer number to get valid address. We can even subtract two addresses but we cannot add two addresses.

Adding Integer with Pointer Value

In C Programming we can add any integer number to Pointer variable. It is legal in c programming to add integer to pointer variable.

For this we have to use following formula:

UNIT-IV Array & Functions

```
Answer = (address) + (number * size of data type) ;
```

Example :

```
int *p , n;
p = &n ;
p = p + 3;
```

Consider the address is 1000.

p = p + 3 * (**sizeof**(integer))
 = 1000 + 3 * (2)
 = 1000 + 6
 = 1006

Similarly we can implement any arithmetic operator like - , * by using above formula (Just change the operator).

Array of Pointers

Like other variable, pointer can be used with array. As we have already discussed array in previous section so in this section we have just use array with pointers.

Syntax:

```
data_type (*var_name)[size_of_array];
```

Example:

```
int (*p)[10];
```

Here ptr is pointer that can point to an array of 10 integers.

Prog # 4.18 Write a program to demonstrate the use of array of pointers.

```
#include <stdio.h>
#include <conio.h>
int main()
    {
    int i;
    int a[5] = {1, 2, 3, 4, 5};
    int *pt = a;              // same as int*pt = &a[0]
    for (i = 0; i < 5; i++)
        {
        printf("%d", *pt);
        p++;
        }
    getch();
    return 0;
    }
```

In the above program, the pointer *pt will print all the values stored in the array one by one. We can also use the Base address to act as a pointer and print all the values.

We can replace the **printf("%d", *pt)** by following statements and that are equals:

   printf ("%d", a[i])

   printf ("%d", a+i)

   printf ("%d", *(a+i))

   printf ("%d", *a)

UNIT-IV   Array & Functions

Calling a function by using call by value

As we have discussed in function introduction section, there are two types of passing values from actual arguments to formal arguments. In call by reference, we have passing the address of actual arguments to formal arguments. In this method, we have not passing the values so in call by reference both actual and formal arguments share the same memory space. Hence, values change inside the function will reflect inside as well as outside the function.

Prog # 4.19 Write a program for swapping by using call by reference.

```
#include <stdio.h>

#include <conio.h>

void swap(int *X, int *Y);

int main()
    {
    int a = 10, b = 15;
    clrscr();
    // address of a and b is passed to the swap function
    swap( &a, &b);
    printf("A = %d\n", a);
    printf("B = %d", b);
    return 0;
    }
void swap(int * X, int * Y)
    {
    // pointer X and Y points to the address of a and b
```

```
    int temp;

    temp = *X;

    *X = *Y;

    *Y = temp;

}
```

OUTPUT

```
A = 15
B = 10
```

- ✓ The address of *a* and *b* are passed to the function swap() and the pointers *X and *Y accept this values.
- ✓ Now, pointer *X* contains the address in memory of variable *a*. And, *Y* contains the address of variable *b*.
- ✓ When the value of pointer variable is changed, the value in the pointed memory location is also changed because both share the same space.
- ✓ Hence, changes made to *x and *Y are reflected in *a* and *b* in the main () function.

Difference between Call by Value & Cal by Reference

Call by Value	Call by Reference
A copy of value is passed to the function	An address of value is passed to the function
Changes made inside the function is not reflected on other functions	Changes made inside the function is reflected outside the function also
Actual and formal arguments	Actual and formal arguments will

will be created in different memory location	be created in same memory location

4.7 Structure Introduction

Structure is the collection of variables of different types under a single name for better handling. For example: You want to store the information about person about his/her name, citizenship number and salary. You can create this information separately but, better approach will be collection of this information under single name because all these information are related to person.

Structure is collection of different data types. For example: We want to store the information about books like Author name , Price , No of pages so for this purpose we use different data items like int ,float , char .So we must have a better programming solutions to combine them that is structure .

Syntax of structure

```
struct structure_name
    {
        data_type member1;
        data_type member2;
            .
            .
        data_type memeber;
    };
```

We can create the structure for a person as mentioned above as:

```
struct Person
{
    char Name[50];
    int Age;
    float Salary;
};
```

This declaration above creates the derived data type struct Person.

Structure variable declaration

When a structure is defined, it creates a user-defined type but, no storage is allocated. For the above structure of person, variable can be declared as:

```
struct person
{
    char Name[50];
    int Age;
    float Salary;
};
```

Inside main function:

struct Person p1, p2;

Another way of creating structure variable is:

```
struct Person
{
    char Name[50];
    int Age;
    float Salary;
} p1 ,p2 ,p[20];
```

In both cases, 2 variables *p1*, *p2* of type **struct person** are created.

Accessing members of a structure

We can use Dot (.) operator for accessing members of a structure.

Any member of a structure can be accessed as: structure_variable_name.member_name

Suppose, we want to access Age, Salary for variable *p2*. Then, it can be accessed as:

p2.Age & p2.Salary

Prog # 4.20 Write a program for use of structure.

```
#include <stdio.h>
#include <conio.h>
struct Student
    {
        char Name[50];
        int Roll;
        float Marks;
    } S;                    // S is structure variable
int main()
    {
        printf("Enter information:\n");
        printf("Enter Name: ");
        scanf("%s", &S.Name);
        printf("Enter roll number: ");
```

```c
    scanf("%d", &S.Roll);
    printf("Enter marks: ");
    scanf("%f", &S.Marks);
    printf("Displaying Information:\n");
    printf("Name: ");
    puts(S.Name);
    printf("Roll number: %d\n",S.Roll);
    printf("Marks: %.1f\n", S.Marks);
    getch();
    return 0;
}
```

OUTPUT

```
Enter information:

Enter name: Garv

Enter roll number: 001

Enter marks: 85.5

Displaying Information:

Name: Garv

Roll number: 001
```

UNIT-IV Array & Functions

Marks: 85.5

UNIT - V

FILE HANDLING & GRAPHICS PROGRAMMING

5.1 File Handling Introduction

File stores information for many purposes and retrieve whenever required by our programs. A file represents a sequence of bytes on the disk where a group of related data is stored. File is created for permanent storage of data and if we want to store large amount of data. The collection of bytes may be interpreted, for example, as characters, words, lines, paragraphs and pages from a textual document; fields and records belonging to a database; or pixels from a graphical image. The meaning attached to a particular file is determined entirely by the data structures and operations used by a program to process the file.

There are two kinds of file exist:

- ✓ ASCII Text File
- ✓ Binary File

ASCII Text File

A text file can be a stream of characters that a computer can process sequentially. It is not only processed sequentially but only in forward direction. For this reason a text file is usually opened for only one kind of operation (reading, writing) at any given time.

Similarly, since text files only process characters, they can only read or write data one character at a time. (In C Programming Language, Functions are provided that deal with lines of text, but these still essentially process data one character at a time.) A text stream in C is a special kind of file. Depending on the requirements of the operating system, newline characters may be converted to or from carriage-return/linefeed combinations depending on whether data is being written to, or read from, the file.

Binary File

A binary file is no different to a text file. It is a collection of bytes. In C Programming Language a byte and a character are equivalent. Hence a binary file is also referred to as a character stream, but there are two essential differences.

1. No special processing of the data occurs and each byte of data is transferred to or from the disk unprocessed.
2. C Programming Language places no constructs on the file, and it may be read from, or written to, in any manner chosen by the programmer.

Binary files can be either processed sequentially or, depending on the needs of the application, they can be processed using random access techniques. In C Programming Language, processing a file using random access techniques involves moving the current file position to an appropriate place in the file before reading or writing data. This indicates a second characteristic of binary files. They a generally processed using read and writes operations simultaneously.

For achieving file handling, in C we need follow following steps:

- ✓ Naming a file
- ✓ Opening a file

- ✓ Reading data from file
- ✓ Writing data into file
- ✓ Closing a file

Functions use in File Handling

Function	Operation
fopen()	To create a file
fclose()	To close an existing file
getc()	Read a single character from a file
putc()	write a single character in file.
fscanf()	Reads a set of data from file
fprintf()	Write a set of data to file
getw()	Read a integer from file
putw()	Write a integer to file
fseek()	Set the position to desire point in file
ftell()	Gives current position to file

Working and Opening a File

As we have discussed in previous section, we must require a file location and for this purpose, we always use pointer variable. So before opening, closing or any operation, we must declare a file pointer variable.

FILE *fpt;

After declaring a file pointer, we can create or open a file by using following syntax:

fpt= fopen("FileName", "Mode")

Where,

File name is actual path or location of your file. It is always local drive in system.

Mode declares the type of operation performed on file. There are several different types of available mode:

Mode	Description
r	opens a text file in reading mode
w	opens or create a text file in writing mode.
a	opens a text file in append mode

r+	opens a text file in both reading and writing mode
w+	opens a text file in both reading and writing mode
a+	opens a text file in both reading and writing mode
rb	opens a binary file in reading mode
wb	opens or create a binary file in writing mode
ab	opens a binary file in append mode
rb+	opens a binary file in both reading and writing mode
wb+	opens a binary file in both reading and writing mode
ab+	opens a binary file in both reading and writing mode

Closing a File

It is always important to close a file after performing reading and writing operation on it. For this we must use following syntax:

fclose(filepointer variable);

fclose(fpt);

File Programs Example

Prog# 5.1: Write any number into file.

```
#include <stdio.h>
#include <conio.h>
void main()
   {
    int No;
    FILE *fpt;                              //File pointer declaration
    fpt = fopen("C:\\Number.txt","w");  // Number is file name
    if(fpt == NULL)                         //Check file is empty
      {
       printf("Error!");
       break;;
      }
    printf("Enter the Number:: ");
    scanf("%d",&No);
    fprintf(fpt,"%d",No);              // Print on file
    fclose(fptr);
```

}

Prog# 5.2 Write a program to storing employee information onto file.

```c
#include <stdio.h>
void main()
   {
    FILE *fpt;
    int ID;
    char Name[30];
    float salary;
    fpt = fopen("emp.txt", "w+");/* open for writing */
    if (fpt == NULL)
      {
        printf("File does not exists \n");
        return;
      }
    printf("Enter the id\n");
    scanf("%d", &ID);
    fprintf(fpt, "Id= %d\n", ID);
    printf("Enter the name \n");
    scanf("%s", &Name);
    fprintf(fpt, "Name= %s\n", Name);
    printf("Enter the salary\n");
    scanf("%f", &salary);
    fprintf(fpt, "Salary= %.2f\n", salary);
```

```
    fclose(fptr);
}
```

Output

```
Enter the ID
1
Enter the name
Garv
Enter the salary
1500000
```

5.2 Graphics Programming

In C programming, it is possible to create a program using graphics. By the help of graphics, we can create any shape, shape with color and also little animation is also possible. For this, we must use some special functions and header file.

By using **graphics.h** header file, we can make programs, animations and also games. For graphics programming we must initialize the graphics driver on our computer. You should know the function initgraph which is used to initialize the graphics mode. To initialize graphics mode we use initgraph function in our program. Initgraph function is present in "graphics.h" header file. Other that initgraph, there are some functions may be used:

- ✓ **delay(n):** A function from dos.h header file is responsible for holding of the program for a while depending upon given value n.
- ✓ **setcolor(n):** A function from graphics.h header file which set the color of pointer(cursor).
- ✓ **arc(x,y,a1,a2,r):** A function from graphics.h header file which draw an arc with (x,y) as centre (a2-a1) as angle and r as radius.

*graphdriver

It contains an integer value that specifies the graphics driver to be used. You can give graphdriver a value using a constant of the graphics drivers enumeration type which is listed in graphics.h . Normally we use value as "0" (requests auto-detect). Other values are 1 to 10.

*graphmode

This is an integer value that specifies the initial graphics mode (unless *graphdriver = DETECT). If*graphdriver = DETECT , then initgraph() method sets *graphmode to the highest resolution available for the detected graphics driver.

Graphics Program Example

```
#include<graphics.h>
#include<conio.h>
void main()
    {
      int gd = DETECT, gm;
```

```
    initgraph(&gd, &gm, "C:\\TC\\BGI");
    getch();
    closegraph();
}
```

Explanation

We have used two variables of int type gd (graphic driver) and gm (graphic mode), you can choose any other variable name. DETECT is a macro defined in "graphics.h" header file, then we have passed three arguments to initgraph function first is the address of gd, second is the address of gm and third is the path where your BGI files are present (You can set your own path where turbo c is installed). Initgraph function automatically decides an appropriate graphics driver and mode such that maximum screen resolution is set, getch helps us to wait until a key is pressed, closegraph function closes the graphics mode.

Prog# 5.3: Write down a graphics program to draw a circle.

```
#include<graphics.h>
#include<conio.h>
void main()
    {
    int gd=DETECT,gm;
    initgraph(&gd,&gm," C:\\TC\\BGI ");   /* initialization of graphic mode */
    circle(150,150,100);              // circle (x ,y , radius)
    getch();
    closegraph();
    }
```

Prog# 5.4: Write down a graphics program to draw a line & rectangle.

```
#include<graphics.h>
#include<conio.h>
void main()
    {
     int gd = DETECT, gm,
left=100,top=100,right=200,bottom=200 ;
        initgraph(&gd,&gm," C:\\TC\\BGI ");
        rectangle(left, top, right, bottom);
        line(left - 10, top + 150, left + 410, top + 150);
        getch();
        closegraph();
    }
```

Prog# 5.5: Write down a graphics program to draw a ellips.

```
#include<graphics.h>
#include<conio.h>
void main()
    {
     int gd = DETECT, gm,
left=100,top=100,right=200,bottom=200 , x =300, y=150;
        initgraph(&gd, &gm," C:\\TC\\BGI ");
        ellipse(x, y + 200, 0, 360, 100, 50);
```

getch();

closegraph();

}

Prog# 5.6: Write down a graphics program to draw a circle with yellow and red color.

```
#include<graphics.h>
#include<conio.h>
void main()
    {
    int gd=DETECT,gm;
    initgraph(&gd,&gm," C:\\TC\\BGI ");   /* initialization of graphic mode */
    setcolor(RED);
    circle(150,150,100);                  // circle (x ,y , radius)
    setcolor(YELLOW);
    circle(250,250,100);
    getch();
    closegraph();
    }
```

APPENDIX- I
OBJECTIVE QUESTIONS

1. Who is father of C programming language?
   - A.) Bjarne Stroustrup
   - B.) James A.Gosling
   - C.) Dennis Ritchie
   - D.) Dr. E. F Codd

2. What is size of Integer data type (For 16-bit Machine)?
   - B.) 2 Bytes
   - B.) 4 Bytes
   - C.) 1 Bytes
   - D.) 6 Bytes

3. Which of the following is not a keyword in C programming language:
   - C.) for
   - B.) if
   - C.) then
   - D.) while

4. Which among the following is an Unconditional Control Structure?
   - D.) for
   - B.) if
   - C.) goto
   - D.) while

5. Array is the collection of:
   - A.) Different Data Types
   - B.) Same Data Types
   - C.) Both Data Types
   - D.) NONE

6. Which of the following symbol is used to denote a preprocessor statement:
   - A.) #
   - B.) !
   - C.) ~
   - D.) <>

7. Default return type of function is:
   - A.) Void
   - B.) int
   - C.) char
   - D.) NONE

Appendix- I   Objective Questions

8. The address of variable can be obtain using operator:
   A.) *   B.) &
   C.) ?   D.) &&

9. If a integer variable a=7/2, then it will store value in a:
   A.) 3.5   B.) 3
   C.) 1   D.) 0

10. C is a type of programming language:
    A.) High level   B.) Middle level
    C.) Low level   D.) NONE

11. Through C program, following file can be created:
    A.) Text File   B.) Binary File
    C.) Decimal File   D.) Both A & B

12. C is a case sensitive language?
    A.) YES   B.) NO

13. Auto Storage class variable is created in:
    A.) Register   B.) Primary Memory
    C.) Secondary Memory   D.) Cache Memory

14. Which of the following is not a type of storage class in C:
    A.) auto   B.) extern
    C.) Static   D.) NONE

15. scanf() function is used for:
    A.) Input   B.) output
    C.) clear the screen   D.) Screen Hold

16. In C programming, Minimum number of function are:
    A.) 0   B.) 1
    C.) 2   D.) 3

17. printf() function is used for:
    A.) input   B.) output
    C.) clear the screen   D.) Screen Hold

18. Break statement is used to:
    A.) Exit from loop   B.) Exit from program
    C.) Exit from switch   D.) NONE

19. In switch expression, which of the following data type cannot be used:
    A.) int   B.) float
    C.) char   D.) long

20. Statement that transfer control to the beginning of the loop is:
    A.) break   B.) continue
    C.) goto   D.) NONE

21. A C variable name can start with a ____
    A.) Number   B.) Plus Sign (+)
    C.) Underscore   D.) Asterisk (*)

22. Name the loop that executes at least once.
    A.) For   B.) If
    C.) do-while   D.) while

23. Which of the following is an example of compounded assignment statement?

   A.) a = 5   B.) a += 5   C.) a = b = c   D.) a = b

24. Which escape character can be used to begin a new line in C?

   A.) \a   B) \b   C.) \m   D.) \n

25. Which operator has the highest priority?

   A.) ++   B.) %   C.) +   D.) |

ANSWER KEY

1.	C	6.	A	11.	D	16.	B	21.	C
2.	A	7.	A	12.	A	17.	B	22.	C
3.	C	8.	B	13.	B	18.	A	23.	C
4.	C	9.	B	14.	D	19.	B	24.	D
5.	B	10.	B	15.	A	20.	B	25.	B

www.ingramcontent.com/pod-product-compliance
Lightning Source LLC
Chambersburg PA
CBHW071500040426
42444CB00008B/1431